UNEXPECTED GAINS

Tavistock Clinic Series

Margot Waddell (Series Editor)
Published and distributed by Karnac Books

Other titles in the Tavistock Clinic Series

Acquainted with the Night: Psychoanalysis and the Poetic Imagination
Hamish Canham and Carole Satyamurti (editors)

Assessment in Child Psychotherapy
Margaret Rustin and Emanuela Quagliata (editors)

Facing It Out: Clinical Perspectives on Adolescent Disturbance
Robin Anderson and Anna Dartington (editors)

Inside Lives: Psychoanalysis and the Growth of the Personality
Margot Waddell

Internal Landscapes and Foreign Bodies:
Eating Disorders and Other Pathologies
Gianna Williams

Mirror to Nature: Drama, Psychoanalysis, and Society
Margaret Rustin and Michael Rustin

Multiple Voices: Narrative in Systemic Family Psychotherapy
Renos K. Papadopoulos and John Byng-Hall (editors)

Psychoanalysis and Culture: A Kleinian Perspective
David Bell (editor)

Psychotic States in Children
Margaret Rustin, Maria Rhode, Alex Dubinsky, Hélène Dubinsky (editors)

Reason and Passion: A Celebration of the Work of Hanna Segal
David Bell (editor)

Sent Before My Time: A Child Psychotherapist's View of
Life on a Neonatal Intensive Care Unit
Margaret Cohen

Surviving Space: Papers on Infant Observation.
Essays on the Centenary of Esther Bick
Andrew Briggs (editor)

Therapeutic Care for Refugees: No Place Like Home
Renos K. Papadopoulos (editor)

Understanding Trauma: A Psychoanalytic Approach
Caroline Garland (editor)

Orders
Tel: +44 (0)20 8969 4454; Fax: +44 (0)20 8969 5585
Email: shop@karnacbooks.com
www.karnacbooks.com

UNEXPECTED GAINS
Psychotherapy with People with Learning Disabilities

edited by
David Simpson & Lynda Miller

KARNAC
LONDON   NEW YORK

First published in 2004 by
Karnac Books Ltd.
118 Finchley Road, London NW3 5HT

Copyright © 2004 David Simpson & Lynda Miller

The rights of editors and contributors to be identified as the authors of this work have been asserted in accordance with §§ 77 and 78 of the Copyright Design and Patents Act 1988.

All rights reserved. No part of this publication may be reproduced, stored in a retrieval system, or transmitted, in any form or by any means, electronic, mechanical, photocopying, recording, or otherwise, without the prior written permission of the publisher.

British Library Cataloguing in Publication Data

A C.I.P. for this book is available from the British Library

ISBN 978 1 85575 964 0

10 9 8 7 6 5 4 3 2 1

Edited, designed, and produced by Communication Crafts

www.karnacbooks.com

CONTENTS

ACKNOWLEDGEMENTS ix
SERIES EDITOR'S PREFACE xi
ABOUT THE EDITORS AND CONTRIBUTORS xiii
INTRODUCTION xix

CHAPTER ONE
The psychotherapy of a little girl with a severe learning
disability and a history of deprivation and neglect
Maria Kakogianni 1

CHAPTER TWO
Therapeutic dilemmas when working with a group
of children with physical and learning disabilities
Sally Hodges and Nancy Sheppard 14

CHAPTER THREE
Some thoughts on psychotherapeutic work
with learning-disabled children and their parents
from orthodox religious communities
Judith Usiskin 30

CHAPTER FOUR
Facing the damage together: some reflections
arising from the treatment in psychotherapy
of a severely mentally handicapped child
Louise Emanuel 45

CHAPTER FIVE
Learning disability as a refuge from knowledge
David Simpson 69

CHAPTER SIX
Adolescents with learning disabilities:
psychic structures that are not conducive to learning
Lynda Miller 83

CHAPTER SEVEN
The creative use of limited language in psychotherapy
by an adolescent with a severe learning disability
Annie Baikie 98

CHAPTER EIGHT
The question of a third space in psychotherapy
with adults with learning disabilities
Pauline Lee and Sadegh Nashat 112

CHAPTER NINE
When there is too much to take in:
some factors that restrict the capacity to think
Elisa Reyes-Simpson 122

CHAPTER TEN
An exploration of severe learning disability
in adults and the study of early interaction
Lydia Hartland-Rowe 133

CHAPTER ELEVEN
The endings of relationships between people
with learning disabilities and their keyworkers
Victoria Mattison and Nancy Pistrang 149

CHAPTER TWELVE
Ensuring a high-quality service:
clinical audit, quality assurance, and outcome research
in the Tavistock Clinic Learning Disabilities Service
Nancy Sheppard, Sally Hodges, and Marta Cioeta 167

REFERENCES 187

INDEX 197

ACKNOWLEDGEMENTS

We would first of all like to acknowledge the enormous debt of gratitude that we and all the contributors to this book owe to the people with learning disabilities, and to their families and carers, on whose experience this book is based. We would also like to thank all those people—staff, students, and other colleagues—who have over the years contributed to the development of psychotherapeutic services for people with learning disabilities at the Tavistock Clinic. We would particularly like to thank Nick Temple and Margaret Rustin for the loyal support that they have given to the Tavistock Learning Disabilities Service over the years and for their encouragement to write this book. We would also like to thank Margot Waddell, Series Editor, for her helpful advice with manuscripts. We are, finally, particularly grateful to Maria Fake, our team secretary, for all the work she has done in this production.

Authors of individual chapters would like to acknowledge the following people who have made helpful contributions: Lynda Miller (chapter one); Valerie Sinason (chapters three and four);

Margaret Rustin, Gianna Williams (chapter four); Maria Kakogianni, Edna O'Shaughnessy (chapter six); Barnado's staff for their constant support (chapter seven); Isabel Hernandez Hatton (chapter nine).

SERIES EDITOR'S PREFACE

Since it was founded in 1920, the Tavistock Clinic has developed a wide range of therapeutic approaches to mental health that have been strongly influenced by psychoanalysis. It has also adopted systemic family therapy as a theoretical model and a clinical approach to family problems. The Clinic is the largest training institution in Britain for mental health, providing postgraduate and qualifying courses in social work, psychology, psychiatry, child, adolescent, and adult psychotherapy, as well as in nursing and primary care. It trains about 1,400 students each year in over 45 courses.

The Clinic's philosophy is aimed at promoting therapeutic methods in mental health. Its work is founded on the clinical expertise that is the basis of its consultancy work and research. This series aims to make available the clinical, theoretical, and research work that is most influential at the Tavistock Clinic. It sets out new approaches in the understanding and treatment of psychological disturbance in children, adolescents, and adults, both as individuals and in families.

Unexpected Gains describes the Tavistock's pioneering work with children, adolescents, and adults with different degrees of learning disability and associated mental and emotional problems, nearly a decade on from Valerie Sinason's vastly influential book, *Mental Handicap and the Human Condition*, which drew so significantly on her work at the Tavistock over a number of years. The chapters in this volume draw on, elaborate, and further explore this centrally important tradition of bringing psychoanalytic concepts to bear on the opaque, puzzling, and painful states of mind of the learning disabled referred for psychotherapeutic help. These concepts are drawn from a range of professional experience—in particular, that of insight into the nature of early mother–infant interactions and their special complexities where learning disability is concerned.

The various chapters movingly and challengingly emphasize the impressive changes that can be achieved within the general framework of psychodynamic practice. The approach demonstrates how, through adaptations and innovations of technique, people and institutions can move towards a greater understanding of the almost unbearable difficulties of this group of patients, and also of their potentialities. This is true not only for those individuals who have often suffered abuse, abandonment, trauma, failure of care, and long-term institutionalization, but also for groups of children and the organizational settings where they are cared for. The "unexpected gains" of the title result from the work of an extraordinarily dedicated multidisciplinary and mutually supportive Service and offers clear and sensitive evidence of the ways in which it is possible to improve the quality of life of even the most deeply disadvantaged.

Margot Waddell
Series Editor

ABOUT THE EDITORS AND CONTRIBUTORS

Annie Baikie trained at the Tavistock Clinic. She currently works as a Child Psychotherapist at the Royal Aberdeen Children's Hospital, where, as well as working for the Department of Child and Family Psychiatry and Psychology's generic teams, she works in both the Specialist Learning Disability Team and the Specialist Looked After, Adopted and Accommodated Children's Team. She teaches locally based courses in the Grampian region for the Scottish Institute of Human Relations. Having previously worked as a drama/movement therapist, she maintains an interest in work with children and adults with limited language and is particularly interested in the interplay of non-verbal communication with the transference–countertransference relationship. She supervises creative art therapists as far apart as London and Orkney. She was recently involved in a series of films at the Glasgow Film Theatre, where issues of childhood were explored from a psychoanalytic perspective.

Marta Cioeta trained as a Psychologist in Italy and in Psychoanalytic Observational Studies at the Tavistock Clinic, where she is currently training as a Child and Adolescent Psychotherapist and working in the Child and Family Department. Her experience includes working with people with learning disabilities, those affected by eating disorders, and those who suffered abuse. She has worked as counsellor in primary schools, currently within the Tavistock Outreach Project in Schools (TOPS).

Louise Emanuel is a Consultant Child and Adolescent Psychotherapist, working in the Department of Children and Families, Tavistock Clinic, where she runs the Under Fives Service. She has a special interest in working with children with learning disabilities and staff consultation. She is a visiting lecturer in Ireland, South Africa, and Italy. She is currently co-editing a book on therapeutic work with pre-school-age children.

Lydia Hartland-Rowe is a Child and Adolescent Psychotherapist working in a psychotherapy service for adolescents and at the Tavistock Clinic in a teaching capacity. She has worked within services for children, adolescents, and adults with learning disabilities for nearly 20 years, initially as a music therapist and as a residential social worker. She then provided training for staff working within voluntary-sector services for people with learning disabilities as a staff development officer. She has worked as a child psychotherapist with young people with learning disabilities and is currently a tutor on the Tavistock Clinic course relating to psychotherapeutic approaches to learning disability.

Sally Hodges is a Consultant Clinical Psychologist in the Learning Disabilities Service and autism team of the Tavistock Clinic. She has ten years' experience working with children and adults with learning disabilities. She is the organizing tutor for the Tavistock Clinic's postgraduate diploma in psychodynamic approaches to working with people with learning disabilities. She has published papers and book chapters on a range of topics, including autism, child protection, child development, and feeding difficulties, and she is the main author of *Counselling Adults with Learning Disabilities*, published by Palgrave in 2002.

Maria Kakogianni is a Psychologist with the Psychiatric Hospital of Athens currently working in rehabilitation services for people with learning disabilities and psychiatric disorders. Maria also works for the Hellenic Centre for the Mental Health of Children and Families: "Perivolaki", a therapeutic unit for children with autism and pervasive developmental disorders. Maria worked with the Learning Disabilities Service of the Tavistock Clinic from 1995 to 1999. She is currently studying part-time for a PhD, doing research on gender and the emotional development of adolescents with learning disabilities.

Pauline Lee is a Consultant Clinical Psychologist who has specialized in two main areas: the mental health of people with learning disabilities and the clinical psychology of children and adolescents. She trained and worked originally in Canada, where she was jointly responsible for developing the assessment and treatment protocols for a specialist mental health and learning disability team in Vancouver. Her current assessment and therapeutic work includes a combination of psychiatric, psychotherapeutic, and behavioural approaches. She is currently head of clinical psychology services for people with learning disabilities at the Cheshire and Wirral NHS Partnership.

Victoria Mattison is a Clinical Psychologist working with adults with learning disabilities in Tower Hamlets, London. Since completing her clinical training and specialist learning disability placement at the Tavistock Clinic in 1998, she has worked with children and adults with learning disabilities, and young people at risk of exclusion from school. Victoria has recently returned to the Tavistock to complete a diploma in Systemic Work with Families. She has published two papers about working with adults with learning disabilities and has co-authored one book, *Saying Goodbye: When Keyworker Relationships End* (with Nancy Pistrang).

Lynda Miller is joint Head of the Tavistock Clinic Learning Disabilities Service and Consultant Child and Adolescent Psychotherapist in the Adolescent Department of the Tavistock Clinic. She also works as Principal Child and Adolescent Psychotherapist in the Child Guidance Service in Enfield. She teaches on pre-clinical and clinical training courses at the Tavistock and in Bologna, Italy, and has published papers in the United Kingdom and in Italy.

Sadegh Nashat is a Chartered Clinical Psychologist who initially trained at the University of Geneva. He has done further training at the Institute of Psychology in Paris in personality assessment and projective techniques and has a particular interest in ethno-cultural issues in psychotherapy. He is currently working at the Tavistock Clinic in partnership with the Camden Local Education Authority Behaviour Support Service, working mainly with children who are at risk of permanent exclusion and with their families.

Nancy Pistrang is a Senior Lecturer in Clinical Psychology at University College London. She obtained her PhD in clinical psychology from UCLA, after which she worked as a clinical psychologist in the British National Health Service before taking up her present position. Her research focuses on psychological helping in everyday relationships, including communication in couples, non-professional helping, and mutual support groups. In addition to publishing in a range of psychological journals, she has co-authored two books, *Research Methods in Clinical Psychology* (with Chris Barker and Robert Elliott) and *Saying Goodbye: When Keyworker Relationships End* (with Victoria Mattison).

Elisa Reyes-Simpson is an Adult Psychotherapist and a Senior Lecturer in Social Work at the Tavistock Clinic. Following a degree in psychology and experience of working with adolescents, she undertook a masters' degree at the Centre for Contemporary Cultural Studies at Birmingham University. After training in social work, she worked in adult mental health. She also has a private psychotherapy practice.

Nancy Sheppard is a Clinical Psychologist working in the Learning Disabilities Service and Children and Families Department at the Tavistock Clinic. She has worked with adults and children with learning disabilities since qualifying as a Clinical Psychologist in 1996 and currently organizes the learning disabilities module on the University of East London Doctorate in Clinical Psychology course. She is also involved in the Post-Graduate Certificate in Working Psychodynamically with People with Learning Disabilities set up and run by the Learning Disabilities Service at the Tavistock Clinic. She is course organizer for specialist placement in clinical psychology and has published several papers and reviews relating to working with people with learning disabilities. She has contributed three chapters to *Counselling Adults with Learning Disabilities*, published by Palgrave in 2003.

David Simpson is joint Head of the Tavistock Clinic Learning Disabilities Service. Following a background in paediatrics, he trained in psychiatry at the Maudsley Hospital. He is a Consultant Child and Adolescent Psychiatrist and Programme Director for Specialist Training in Child and Adolescent Psychiatry at the Tavistock Clinic and is Honorary Senior Lecturer at the Royal Free and University College London Hospital Medical School. He is a Member of the British Psychoanalytic Society and works in private practice as a psychoanalyst.

Judith Usiskin trained as a Child and Adolescent Psychotherapist at the Tavistock Clinic. She has been a member of the Learning Disabilities Service since its inception, and she has lectured and taught widely, both in the United Kingdom and abroad, on working with people with learning disabilities. She divides her time between the Tavistock Learning Disabilities Service and the Young Abusers Project, a forensic psychotherapy resource offering assessment and treatment for children and adolescents with sexually harmful behaviour.

INTRODUCTION

Until recently, psychotherapy would not have been considered a treatment option for those people who have both learning disabilities and mental health problems. Traditionally, the treatment of emotional and behavioural difficulties within the population of people with learning disabilities has been at the level of behavioural management combined with skills teaching and medical approaches (Waitman & Conboy-Hill, 1992). Counselling, in the general sense of sympathetic listening and advice giving, has also been available, but psychoanalytic psychotherapy is a fairly recent development.

This book reflects the clinical and consultative work of the members of staff of the Learning Disabilities Service at the Tavistock Clinic in North London. This service began in 1995, with the aim of providing psychoanalytic psychotherapy for children, adolescents, and adults with learning disabilities. The service consists of a specialist multidisciplinary team drawn from psychology, psychiatry, child and adolescent psychotherapy, adult psychotherapy, and social work, who offer assessment and treatment within a psychoanalytic framework. The therapeutic treatment is predominantly that of individual psychotherapy but also includes group work, parent work, family therapy, and consultative work with professionals.

The development of the Learning Disabilities Service can best be understood in the context of the emergence of psychoanalytic psychotherapy as a treatment choice for people with learning disabilities in the United Kingdom, as reflected in training and practice. A survey of psychologists working in the United Kingdom recently identified that as many as 41% consider themselves to have some competency in working psychodynamically with clients with learning disabilities (Nagel & Leiper, 1999).

Interest in working psychoanalytically with people with learning disabilities at the Tavistock Clinic began in 1979, when Neville Symington, a clinical psychologist and psychoanalyst in the Adult Department, treated a man with a mild learning disability. This led him to convene a workshop for therapists who had an interest in this area of work. In his paper (Symington, 1981) he explored the theoretical aspects of the case and posed important questions: What is intelligence? Where is it rooted? In what way can it be damaged organically? And even if damaged, can psychotherapy help to restore the efficiency of intelligence? Symington believed that despair is a central problem:

> There is a strong tendency for people to despair as soon as the word organic is mentioned. The therapist has become more convinced that unwanted despair on the part of those engaged in helping mental defectives is a far greater handicap than the organic defects. Neurological growth can be stimulated and is not static. What remains static are people's expectations that change can occur. [p. 199]

He thought that there should be a greater use of psychoanalytic therapy as a method of treatment for people with learning disabilities.

In 1985, Valerie Sinason, a child psychotherapist, joined Symington in convening this workshop, and the interest within both the Clinic and the field grew (Sinason & Stokes, 1992). This was increased by the courses developed at the Clinic and by staff publications, especially Sinason's (1992b) book, *Mental Handicap and the Human Condition*. She developed the important concept of secondary handicap—a term that refers to the particular use that the person makes of any original organic or traumatic damage (Sinason, 1986). In her view, two elements underlie each IQ score: one is the organic limit of intelligence and the other is secondary handicap, which results from attacks on skills and intelligence as a way of coping with the handicap. Sinason elaborated this view with the belief that, added to the original handicap, there can be a severe personality maldevelopment which further limits intelligence. This is a defensive "stupidity" that originates in the feelings and beliefs of disabled people themselves and in the reactions of others to them.

Jon Stokes, another member of the workshop at that time, also published some important ideas about secondary handicap. Stokes (1987) thought that it was useful to distinguish cognitive from emotional intelligence. Although there is a relationship between the two, his view was that this was not a one-to-one correlation, and he highlighted the depth of emotionality—particularly the capacity to feel psychological pain—that many people with learning disabilities show.

As the influence of the workshop grew, a decision was made to create a separate team that would be able to take referrals from any geographical distance within reason and be staffed by professionals experienced in working psychodynamically with people with learning disabilities.

There is now compelling evidence for the efficacy of this approach. In 1996, Sheila Bichard, a psychologist and founder member of the service, published a paper with Valerie Sinason and Judith Usiskin, a child psychotherapist, in which they demonstrated that patients undergoing long-term weekly individual and group psychotherapy showed an improvement in their symptoms and in measures of social interaction, as well as in measures of cognitive functioning that include an emotional dimension (Bichard, Sinason, & Usiskin, 1996). This is a very important finding that points to further research. There is, however, little published literature on the outcome of psychotherapy with learning-disabled people, as discovered by Beail (1995) when he reviewed the subject. Clearly, more is needed.

Most contemporary psychoanalytic psychotherapists consider that their work is to make contact with their patients' emotional experience in the "here and now" of the session. This is done by closely observing their patients' behaviour, including their speech (if any), and, particularly, by observing within themselves the feelings that are evoked in them by their patients. By following countertransference feelings closely over time, the therapist can build up a picture of the transference: a living memory of the patient's early relationships with important figures, experienced in the here-and-now relationship with the therapist. It is through the transference that change and development can be effected. This can only take place when there is an active emotional understanding in an alive and real relationship between patient and therapist. These principles apply to patients of all ages, including those with learning disabilities.

There are, of course, other developments in this field throughout the United Kingdom and abroad, but they are patchy and few and far between. Practitioners are often clinical psychologists whose general professional training includes a module on learning disability that can lead to specialization. However, the introduction of psychodynamic ideas is rare and is, at best, a very small component of their training: it is usually cognitive behaviour therapy that is emphasized.

In child psychotherapy training, supervised clinical work with children and adolescents with learning disabilities may feature, but rarely is this the case. Experience with autistic children does facilitate therapeutic work in the field of learning disability, since there is often an overlap between the two conditions. Similarly, experience of working with non-verbal children can help psychotherapists to develop useful skills for learning disability cases.

Psychiatrists specializing in work with learning-disabled patients have also recently begun to show an interest in the usefulness of psychotherapy and psychodynamic ideas. In 2002 specialist registrars in learning disability psychiatry held a national conference in Oxford on this theme.

The issue of training, of enabling interested professionals to extend their skills and understanding in a way that makes them feel competent to undertake therapeutic work with people with learning disabilities, is highly pertinent if this work is to continue to flourish. One of the aims of this book is to encourage an interest in training in psychotherapy with this patient group.

There can be an unconscious aversion among people training as psychotherapists and psychodynamic counsellors to taking on patients with learning disabilities. This can be based on a fear that they may be unable to engage with this patient group—a fear that is, in part, socially conditioned. We are all aware of the fact that people with learning disabilities are frequently socially and educationally excluded from the cultural main stream. This is, in itself, a complex phenomenon, but it certainly exists and could—indeed, can—be addressed by developments in training.

Another important issue is the need for careful assessment for suitability for psychotherapy by a specialist multidisciplinary team, who can also provide psychological testing, psychiatric assessment, and social work consultation, as appropriate. This is a resource issue and at present is not widely available. The specialist Learning Disabilities Service at the Tavistock Clinic is among the limited number of existing provisions of this kind, and a further aim of this book is to increase knowledge in this field, thereby encouraging similar developments elsewhere.

Some concepts central to the theme of this book reoccur in different contexts, related to each author's particular focus. The concept of early trauma is referred to in a number of the chapters, especially in the form of the traumatic impact on parents when they give birth to a disabled infant. Some of the authors discuss the various ways in which this can impact upon the early development of a young child with a disability, utilizing a psychodynamic model in which developmental processes are seen as arising out of the complexities of the parent-child relationship.

Another concept referred to frequently in the chapters that follow is that of "secondary handicap" as coined by Sinason (1992b). Secondary handicap can be defined as a process that arises when the original disability is exaggerated as a way of defending the self against the painful feeling of being "different" from the non-learning-disabled population. By means of this process, the learning-disabled person gains a fantasized control over the disability (Hodges, 2003).

This leads on to another central theme that appears throughout this book. All the authors, in describing their clinical work with this patient group, convey the sheer painfulness to all concerned of having a learning disability, and the extent of the defensive manoeuvres used by people to evade this reality.

The chapters in this book reflect the range of psychodynamically informed work that has been undertaken by members of the Learning Disabilities Service since its formation in 1995. The chapters are organized in a way that shows some of the clinical possibilities of therapeutic work with children (chapters one to four), with adolescents (chapters five to eight), and with adults (chapter nine). The last three chapters focus on issues pertinent to psychotherapeutic clinical work, looking at aspects of life in residential settings and at audit and research.

Chapter one is an account by Maria Kakogianni, a clinical psychologist from Greece, who spent some years in London undertaking clinical work for the Learning Disabilities Service, of her work with a little girl with severe learning disability and very limited language, seen in once-weekly psychoanalytic psychotherapy for just over one year. It is evident in this work that deprivation and neglect in the child's early life have contributed to her considerable difficulties.

Sally Hodges and Nancy Sheppard are both clinical psychologists who have contributed significantly to the clinical training and research activities of the Learning Disabilities Service. In chapter two they give a moving account of their school-based work of running a therapeutic group for children who have terminal physical illnesses and learning disabilities. They describe their thoughts about therapeutic technique in relation to this highly sensitive work.

In chapter three, Judith Usiskin, a child and adolescent psychotherapist, describes her work with learning-disabled children and their parents from three different orthodox religious communities: Muslim, Jewish, and Christian. Using sensitive clinical illustrations, she highlights the importance of religion, both as a supportive social structure and sometimes, too, as a vehicle of inhibition and even of abuse. She shows the constraints that patients' religious beliefs can impose on their psychotherapists, but she also conveys how rewarding this work can be when the significance of this is understood.

Louise Emanuel, a child and adolescent psychotherapist who teaches on the course linked to the Learning Disabilities Service, explores, in chapter four, ideas about the nature of the attachment between a mother and her handicapped or damaged baby. These thoughts are illustrated by detailed case material of a 6-year-old severely mentally handicapped girl (brain-damaged at birth).

David Simpson, child and adolescent psychiatrist, psychoanalyst, and joint Head of the Learning Disabilities Service, proposes, in chapter five, that learning disability can become a refuge from knowledge and as such can be an important factor in preventing a person's learning and development. He suggests that the very term "learning disability", through obscuring the distinction between organic and psychological difficulties, can become a refuge from facing the realities of damage and deficiency. From a psychoanalytic perspective he discusses how the emotional consequences of a child's handicap can inhibit curiosity. He illustrates these ideas in his work with an adolescent boy.

In chapter six Lynda Miller, child and adolescent psychotherapist and joint Head of the Learning Disabilities Service, writes about clinical work with adolescents with learning disabilities in psychotherapeutic treatment. She offers some thoughts, from a psychoanalytic theoretical perspective, on how certain aspects of the patient's difficulties can be understood and ameliorated, focusing, in particular, on the part played by a destructive superego in the internal world.

Annie Baikie, a child and adolescent psychotherapist ,gives, in chapter seven, a very evocative and personal account of her psychotherapeutic treatment of a severely learning-disabled adolescent young woman. She demonstrates how this woman, who has limited language ability, develops a capacity to speak her mind as she begins to face inevitable losses.

In chapter eight, Pauline Lee and Sadegh Nashat, both clinical psychologists, consider an important problem facing psychotherapists working with learning-disabled patients: namely, the difficulty of achieving adequate therapeutic space to allow for thinking and growth. They propose that many people with learning disabilities lack the capacity for a psychic third dimension, a concept that they derive from Britton's notion of triangular space (1989). They integrate these ideas with those of Bion and Lacan and suggest that this problem arises from a failure of early maternal containment. They further suggest that this may be a consequence of the mother's failure both to identify with her learning-disabled infant and also to maintain an internal link with the father.

Elisa Reyes-Simpson, an adult psychotherapist and social worker, makes the observation in chapter nine that close contact with people with learning disabilities in psychotherapy can be very difficult for both the psychotherapist and the patient. She proposes that this is indicative of the problem that learning-disabled infants and their mothers frequently have in making contact, as a result of the difficulty they face in taking in and bearing the facts of disability. The consequence of this emotional problem is further intellectual and personality restriction.

In chapter ten, Lydia Hartland-Rowe, a child and adolescent psychotherapist teaching on the training course linked to the Learning Disabilities Service, draws upon her past experience as a music therapist and residential social worker in a therapeutic home for learning-disabled adults with emotional and behavioural difficulties. She discusses ideas about the part played by the early interaction between parent and infant in the development of cognitive ability from psychoanalytic and child development perspectives.

Victoria Mattison's chapter was written in conjunction with Nancy Pistrang, her tutor at University College, London. Chapter eleven is drawn from her thesis for the doctorate in clinical psychology which she was writing during her clinical placement in the Learning Disabilities Service. The focus is on a central aspect of the life of many people with learning disabilities who live in residential settings: that of their relationship with their keyworkers and, in particular, the significance of the ending of this relationship when the keyworker leaves.

Nancy Sheppard, Sally Hodges, and Marta Cioeta provide us, in chapter twelve, with an overview of clinical audit, quality assurance, and outcome research into the provision of psychotherapy for people with learning disabilities. They explore some of the methods available for the assessment and evaluation of this work and describe some important projects, both undertaken and planned, for patients treated in the Tavistock Learning Disabilities Service.

It is hoped that this book will be of interest to a wide range of professionals engaged in therapeutic work with people with learning disabilities and also to students and practitioners of psychotherapy in general. Our wish is that it should be accessible to anyone who is engaged with issues related to learning disability—a wider audience that may include carers, keyworkers, family members, and friends of learning-disabled people.

UNEXPECTED GAINS

CHAPTER ONE

The psychotherapy of a little girl with a severe learning disability and a history of deprivation and neglect

Maria Kakogianni

"Janet" was a learning-disabled little girl whom I saw in once-weekly psychotherapy for a little more than a year. She was referred to the Clinic by social services, who requested an assessment for psychotherapy and help in planning for her future. At that time she was 7 years old and had been in care since the age of 3. The referrer described her as a loveable little girl who displayed indiscriminate affection but could become difficult to control and aggressive when she did not have the full attention of an adult or when she had to cope with minor frustrations. Janet had a severe learning disability and was only able to use a few words. At the time of referral she was placed in a school for children with moderate learning difficulties, but social services were concerned about the suitability of this placement for her needs.

There had been concerns about Janet's development since the time of her birth. In her early childhood she lived with her parents, who both had mild learning difficulties, and with her two older siblings. According to reports from social services, the children were physically and emotionally neglected, and mother's contact with them was almost totally absent. It seemed that Janet and her siblings had started life in an extremely deprived environment. By the time they were taken into care, all the children were seriously underweight, and none of them was able to converse. In their report, social services mentioned concerns about possible physical or sexual abuse of the children, which were, however, never substantiated. After having been removed from their family, Janet and her siblings lived in a children's home for two years. By the time she was referred to the Clinic, Janet had been separated from her brother and sister and placed with short-term foster parents. She had not seen her mother or father in two years and only saw her older brother once a month.

Information on Janet's past made me wonder how this little girl, who had a severe learning disability, could have made sense of a life that so far had been a long string of absences, separations, and losses. Our team were concerned that her external circumstances were so unstable that setting up therapy might be impossible. However, two months before the beginning of Janet's assessment, a permanent foster placement was found for her. Although it was still early days, it seemed that since she had settled with Mrs L, a warm, caring woman, Janet had made considerable progress.

The beginning of assessment

I first encountered Janet when she was 8 years old, in a meeting with her foster mother and social worker. My impressions of her were of a rather small but overweight bubbly and lively little girl, who at the same time seemed very anxious and tense. After my colleague and I introduced ourselves, she was eager to follow us to the room, showing excitement and curiosity about the closed doors as we walked along the corridor. Once in the room, she went straight for the toy box and explored its contents, laughing excitedly. This, however, lasted only for a few minutes, and after quickly flicking through the family of dolls and the farm animals, she seemed more interested in the Sellotape. She asked me to hold on to the end of one piece of tape, while she would pull hard the other end, until it was cut. She kept on with this pulling and cutting for a while, and I felt there was a desperate quality in her making and breaking of this link between us, which was made more intense by her clumsiness. I felt she was letting me know of her need to connect and at the same time her anxieties about relationships or links being cut off. She turned to the Plasticine and said to me, "I like dinner." She was simultaneously anxiously checking on her foster mother, who was talking to my colleague. She pointed at her and said "Mummy" to me, and I had the feeling she wanted to share with me her excitement about her new Mummy. Towards the end of our meeting she made two little balls of Plasticine and placed one on my head and one on hers. When our time finished, Janet did not want to leave the room, and on her way out she took my hand in hers as if she wanted to take me with her. I said to her that we would meet again the following week, but when I uttered these words, she stared at me lifelessly, and I had the feeling that it was very difficult for her to have a thought of coming back and finding me here. It seemed to me that she needed literally to hold on to me as if I would disappear the minute she was not able to see me any more.

After the meeting ended, I was left with a strong impression that there was something desperate in this little girl's need to connect. I felt that there was something alive in her, a part of her that was able to communicate powerfully her despair about the impossibility of maintaining a link, and that evoked in me an urge to help her. However, her need to latch on to this relationship with me made me think that there was something rather rushed and superficial about her way of forming attachments. She seemed urgently to need to take in a good nurturing object (the therapist and the therapy "food", a new "Mummy"), but her way of relating was of an "adhesive" kind, a precarious sticking to external qualities of this object (Meltzer, 1975a). Clinical reports on young children who have not had an experience of adequate parenting stress their tendency to cling to the therapist and crave for affection in a way that often feels flat and superficial (Boston & Szur, 1983).

Janet's psychotherapy

In her early sessions, Janet let me see more of her urge to make up for lost time, to greedily grab on to things and devour them, and her fear that her needs could not possibly be met. She would come to the room and show no more than a fleeting interest in the toys, preferring instead to spend the time in an endless overflowing of cups and pots with water, as though they were bottomless and could never really stay full. Sometimes, after having looked into the toy box, she would start frantically searching the room for something lost or hidden, climbing on the settee or the table and pulling the furniture so that she could look behind it. She would also use up all the Plasticine, cutting it into small pieces to make what she called "cakes", which she insisted on taking home with her at the end of each session. I felt that for Janet, letting go of her Plasticine "cakes" caused tremendous, unbearable anxiety. When I said that she should leave them with me in the room for our next session, she protested as fiercely as if her life literally depended on these "cakes", making me a cruel, depriving parental figure. At this early stage I found that interpretations focusing on Janet's fear that I could not be trusted to be there and take care of her and "her cakes" were felt to be intrusive and violent. When I made such comments, she would sometimes scream at the top of her voice, so as not to listen to me. I felt that if I insisted on her leaving everything in the room, Janet would experience me as unable to take in her terrified state. At the same time, I was aware that it was important for me not to become over-accommodating, constantly filling up with material an ever-emptying box. I therefore tried to negotiate with her to leave at least one piece of Plasticine in her box, and I avoided replacing the Plasticine as soon as it finished. According to Hunter (2001), a modification of technique is sometimes necessary with children who have experienced deprivation and disruptions of care. These children may find it hard to think that an adult can be relied on to be there and may need to bring or take something from the therapy-room in an attempt "to establish continuity and bridge one session to another" (p. 108).

In a discussion of the feelings aroused in the therapist when working with severely deprived children Hoxter (1983) describes the way the therapist is alternately put in the position of the persecutor (the neglecting parental figure) and the victim (the frightened, needy, abandoned child). During these first months in Janet's therapy, I was often put in the position of a therapy mother who is withholding the "food" or is failing to provide something extremely vital. Many times during one session she would climb on the windowsill or the table in a way that made me worry about her safety, and I had to stand by in case she fell off. It was perhaps her way of communicating her feeling that she was "on the edge", in danger, and wondering whether I would care enough to protect her. She would also make provocative attempts at cutting her shirt with the scissors, putting a piece of Plasticine in her mouth, or running towards the door, while looking at me as if waiting to see whether I would stop her. She usually responded to my comments on how hard it was for her to think that I wanted her to be safe or that I wanted her in the room, and this behaviour gradually stopped. There were other times when I was made to feel powerless or confused. Janet would often order me around the room, one minute asking me to sit down beside her, only to push me away or shout at me "go away" as soon as I had done so. Sometimes I felt overwhelmed by her uncontrollable behaviour in the corridor. A couple of times she ran away from me and tried to open doors along the corridor, and once she lay down and started shouting and rolling on the floor. I felt that I had to be firm with her about what was acceptable and where, so that the room and the session time could begin to serve as a safe container for her overwhelming, frightening states of mind.

Janet was very preoccupied with rubbish and the rubbish bin, and this was a theme that emerged in almost all her sessions throughout the year. She seemed to be extremely and disproportionately worried about what qualifies as rubbish and can be thrown away. She would often throw away tiny pieces of paper, only to retrieve them anxiously a few minutes later and put them back in the toy box. She seemed to find it hard to tell the difference between what is rubbish and what is not, as though she had to hang on to everything in case it got taken away. Mrs L reported that at home Janet tried to stop her whenever Mrs L wanted to throw something away and would constantly retrieve things from the bin. Perhaps this was linked to Janet's feelings that she herself might be rubbish and I (or Mrs L) might wish to throw her away.

Interestingly, her preoccupation with the rubbish bin was most pronounced in the last session before the first break, when she herself literally stepped into the bin.

Terror and the need for containment

Janet seemed to live in a world where extreme states of rage, fear, or excitement were "things in themselves" that could not be thought about and were available only for evacuation (Bion, 1962a). She found it very hard to tolerate the anxiety brought on by these undigested feelings. In the first months of therapy, her only way to manage this anxiety was to ask to go to the toilet—sometimes twice or three times during one session. Sometimes this was after she had wondered aloud where "Mummy" was or when she felt let down by me because her toy box was "empty". At these moments Janet would anxiously repeat that she wanted to "pee" and would at first scream or cover her ears, so that my words could not reach her. Gianna Williams (1997) talks about a "hollow" mental state in many deprived children, a "fragile internal container whose 'floor' easily collapses" (p. 28), that stifles learning by compelling the evacuation of painful thoughts or feelings. I tried to talk to Janet about her wish to get rid of all these terrible feelings, while at the same time I said to her that I thought she could manage to stay in the room until the end of our session.

The therapy-room for Janet seemed to be either the source of good things where cakes could be found or a dark, threatening, but also exciting place that sometimes seemed to cause claustrophobic anxiety. I came to understand this more fully after Session 12, the first after a break that had been longer than planned due to cancellations from Janet's carer.

They arrived about 15 minutes late, and on the way to the therapy-room Janet seemed unusually anxious, running away from me and stopping to look behind and see if I was following her. As soon as she entered the room, she went straight for the toy box, which she opened, saying "cakes" in excited anticipation. This time, however, she only had a glimpse of its contents before closing the lid and placing the box on the floor, saying "no cakes!" I talked about Janet's wish to find that I had kept something good for her during the holidays and also her fear that her toy box would be empty because I had not seen her for a long time. As I was saying this, she climbed on the mantelpiece and sat on it, screaming excitedly and banging her feet on the radiator so as to make a very loud noise. I acknowledged that it had been a very long time since the last time she had seen me, and perhaps she had been wondering whether I liked her enough to want to see her again. She climbed off the mantelpiece, came towards me, and pushed me away angrily. I said that she wanted to tell me how angry she was with me for disappearing during our break and how she had felt I had pushed her away. She turned off the light and closed the curtains. She then climbed on the couch and started frantically jumping up and down and screaming in fear and excitement, looking completely disconnected from me, as if in a trance-like state. I commented on Janet's feeling that I had become a bad Maria who was not there to see her, and that the room was suddenly a dark and frightening place. She kept on jumping, but, as I was talking to her, she stopped screaming and turned to face me, her eyes enlivened with interest. She gradually slowed down her jumping and gave me her hands to hold. I said that perhaps she felt that I could help with those frightening feelings. Janet eventually stopped jumping. She sat on the couch for a while and then turned to her toy box, which she brought to the couch and emptied. She now seemed very calm and curious about the contents of her toy box. She picked up some of the farm animals and wanted me to help her with their names. She said, "I like dinner" and picked up a piece of Plasticine to make a "cake". She then pulled the curtains open and walked to the desk.

This session shows, I think, how in Janet's mind my absence during the break could only be experienced in very concrete terms as "no cakes" or an "empty" box. Her feeling of internal emptiness got confused with external reality. When I tried to make a link and give some meaning to her perception of emptiness, she attacked this link by making loud noises and covering my voice. However, at least momentarily she was in touch with feelings of dependency and her anger at me for "pushing her away", letting her down during the break. She then closed the curtains, turned off the light, and seemed drawn in a phantasy of being inside the "claustrum" (Meltzer, 1992). This phantasy of intrusion in the maternal body can be—sometimes simultaneously—both an attempt to find a safe refuge through omnipotent denial of infantile dependency or a way to experience a "perverse sense of power" (Dubinsky, 1997). During the long minutes of Janet's wild jumping I could feel her terror and excitement both overwhelming her. I was aware that it was not just the content of what I was saying that could help her leave this phantasy, but the very fact that I was talking to her and the tone of my voice. She needed to feel that I could receive the state she was in, including her anger towards me, and survive it, so that I could literally hold her. When this sense of basic trust was established, she was able to return to the world and, for the first time, no matter how briefly, become curious about the toys in the box.

"Waiting"

In the months that followed, some development in Janet slowly became apparent. This was by no means linear, as there were always setbacks and regressions, especially around holidays. She did, however, become increasingly able to accept boundaries and stopped protesting at having to leave the room at the end of each session. She now seemed to have an idea that both myself and the toys would be there for her the following week. She still sometimes needed to take home something concrete with her (usually her Plasticine-made "cakes"), but most of the time she would now accept leaving things in the room with me for next time. It was clear that she was starting to develop a capacity to think that people could wait for her and not disappear and that she herself was a more grown-up girl who could wait and not expect her needs to be instantly gratified. She had now started to be interested in naming the dolls and the animals and playing with the toy phone, in a way that indicated a strong desire to communicate with me in words. Her foster mother, Mrs L, who was considering adopting Janet, felt that she was now easier to manage at home and could tolerate not having what she wanted straight away. At school, however, Janet was still aggressive to other children and would become very agitated when her teacher was attending to them.

This is an excerpt from Session 25, about eight months into her therapy:

> Janet had spent the early part of the session sitting at the desk and cutting a small piece of Plasticine into smaller ones—making "dinner", as she said. She then carried her toy box to a chest of drawers that was at the other side of the room, placed it on top of it, and climbed on it herself. She now began cutting a piece of cardboard, using the scissors. She heard a car horn from the street and started talking as though she were telling me a story. I felt that she really wanted to tell me something and that although her speech was unintelligible, she was actually trying to talk to me in a more grown-up way, so I commented on this. She went on talking like that for a while, until one small piece of cardboard accidentally slipped behind the chest of drawers. Janet instantly became very anxious, got down to the floor, and asked me to help her move the furniture away from the wall so that she could retrieve the piece. I said that she seemed really frightened about losing this little piece of cardboard. She found the piece and then sat down on the floor next to the wall, taking her Plasticine with her. She stuck some small pieces on the wall, saying "nice" and "me", pointing at herself, smiling, and looking at me. I felt she wanted to let me know how pleased she was to have her room and her time with me but that she also wished it could be her room all the time and I would not see another child after her. Although she was absorbed in this for a while, I could see that from time to time she was instantly overtaken by anxiety but was able to contain herself. She asked, "where's Mummy?" looking worried and then replied herself: "waiting". A few moments later she said, "I want toilet" and then immediately she said "wait", as if talking to herself. I said that Janet thought she could wait, she did not have to go to the toilet straight away and get rid of what was upsetting her. She kept on sticking pieces of Plasticine on the wall. It was almost time to finish, and I said so. She then started taking the Plasticine off the wall, scraping off any remaining bits carefully so as to leave it

clean. Janet quickly wrapped up the Plasticine with paper and put it in her pockets. I asked her to leave the Plasticine here for the following week, and although she said no, she took the packets out of her pocket and put them in the box.

Janet now seemed more able to have a concept of me as a live presence in the room. She was still terrified at losing the tiniest bit of paper, as though this would mean literally losing a part of herself. However, she could now contain this anxiety and not let herself slip into a state of diffuse agony over "something" that is irretrievably lost. She also seemed to have a thought of her foster mother "waiting" for her and to trust that I would be there the following week and would look after her "cakes" in the meantime. For Janet, having the beginning of a thought of people waiting meant that they could be alive in her mind: they could exist and be thought of in their absence. This was linked with Janet's ability to bear the anxiety caused by upsetting feelings, thus interrupting the vicious circle of their evacuation as bodily excrements. "Waiting" gave Janet a space where these feelings could begin to be thought about.

Ending

Unfortunately therapeutic work with this little girl came to a premature end. About two months before the end of the first year it became clear that Janet would not be able to continue her therapy. Her local education authority had found a more suitable day school for her, but this involved a long bus journey, so coming to the Clinic was no longer possible. During the last two months the work concentrated on Janet's feelings about the ending. Most of the time during these last sessions she was anxious and tense and had gone back to wanting to grab on to everything and take it home with her. She kept asking me almost constantly if it was "eight o'clock" which was her way of asking if it was time to end the session. She often referred to her toy box as empty and the things inside it as "broken", as if I could no longer give her anything good, given that our relationship would "break" in a few weeks. Three weeks before the end, Janet spent almost the whole session anxiously looking for "cakes" in the room, ignoring the Plasticine and giving me the impression that she was looking for something that could not possibly be found.

She picked up the drawing I had made the week before (three circles representing our remaining sessions). I said to her that she would come here and meet with me three more times before we say good bye. She took the scissors and tried to cut the paper. She said, "broke". I said that Janet was maybe wondering about her therapy, feeling that it too had "broken". She looked in the box again and said, "where's cake?" shrugging her shoulders. I said that she felt the cakes had gone today, disappeared, and maybe she was also thinking about me going. She took the pen and drew three more circles underneath the ones I had drawn. I said she wanted me to know that she wished we had more time together. She looked at me and smiled and for a few seconds seemed very unsure about what to do next. She picked up a piece of Plasticine, looked at it, and threw it back in the box, saying, "I don't like cakes." She then emptied the box on the table and seemed to be looking for something. She continued looking around anxiously and asking me "Where's cake?" I said that she felt that the "cakes" had gone bad today and then she wasn't sure if there was anything good to be found in the room any more. She took my hand and pointed at her eyes, indicating she wanted me to look for "cakes". She then took some Plasticine, the scissors, and glue and sat down on the floor next to the wall. She looked at me and said, "me, cakes", pointing at her chest. She sat down on the floor, cut a few pieces of Plasticine, glued them, and stuck them on the wall. I said she perhaps wished she could stick with me like those "cakes" on the wall. While she was doing this, she turned and looked out the window and said "rain". She got up, drew the curtains close, and said "no rain". I said it seemed she wanted to shut the rain out, and maybe she also wanted to make all the sad feelings go away. She took one piece of Plasticine, climbed on the chair, and tried to stick it as high up on the wall as she could reach . She said, "me", smiling. I said that she stuck this little piece really high, so that no one could take it away, so that it stays here with me and I can think of Janet when she has gone. It was time to finish, and I said so. She anxiously picked up the paper and Plasticine and tried to wrap everything up in a hurry. She refused to leave anything behind."

Conclusion

Janet's complex difficulties illustrate how emotional factors can become deeply intertwined with the development of thought and language and the capacity to learn. At the age of 7, she was a very disturbed little girl, overwhelmed by anxieties linked to her painful history and caught in what seemed to be a vicious circle. Whatever organic deficit Janet was born with, this must have been exacerbated by the lack of a relationship with an adult who could receive her communications and reflect them back to her in a more manageable, digested form (Bion, 1962a). As she was growing up, her difficulties in using language and her extremely limited vocabulary meant that for Janet the experience of not being understood was constantly and painfully re-enacted. Therapy aimed at providing a space where details of her powerful non-verbal and verbal communications could be thought about, named, and understood.

The development of thought is intrinsically linked with the experience of an absent object (Bion, 1962b; O'Shaughnessy, 1964). In an attempt to keep the object (at first the mother's breast) alive while it is away and cope with the frustration caused by its absence, the infant turns the reality of "no breast" to a thought of an absent breast. If the infant has a low capacity for tolerating frustration, the absent object becomes a "bad object, indistinguishable from a thing-in-itself, fit only for evacuation" (Bion, 1962b, p. 307). The development of an inner space where thinking is possible is disturbed, as thoughts and feelings are treated as bad, persecuting objects, only to be manipulated through excessive use of projective identification. Children like Janet who have suffered so many losses and experienced relationships with objects that were too unavailable are more vulnerable to this obliteration of inner space as a defensive strategy in order to get rid of painful thoughts and feelings (Williams, 1997).

Janet's desperate clinging to objects was linked to the end of our time together and the prospect of the gap between sessions and my disappearance. At the beginning, the end of a session was only bearable if she could take something from the room with her. I felt that she was having great difficulty in seeing me as a separate person who could continue to exist in her mind when "out of sight". Clinging to material objects and becoming the possessor of my "cakes" was perhaps her way of denying separation. Gradually, the regularity of the sessions, the repetition of the experience of being lost and found again, made it easier for Janet to "let go" of this omnipotent denial and acquire a sense of object permanence. Only then did curiosity and the desire to learn begin to emerge.

Unfortunately the work stopped when these gains still felt extremely precarious. Janet's world was terribly concrete, and her way of relating still had this "sticking" quality to it, thereby leaving much doubt as to whether it would be possible for her to introject firmly a different type of object. It seemed that long-term work was needed to help her to build on this glimpse of a space where thought was possible, but hopefully some foundations have been put in place.

CHAPTER TWO

Therapeutic dilemmas when working with a group of children with physical and learning disabilities

Sally Hodges and Nancy Sheppard

This chapter concerns a group for children with progressive musculo-skeletal wasting disorders that is run at a main stream secondary school. Initially two members of the group had learning disabilities, two did not. The orientation is that of psychodynamic group therapy, and the therapists are grappling with the dilemma of how much to challenge the children's defences, given the poor prognosis related to their medical conditions. The main issues in running this group are described and explored, specifically the impact of the setting, the use of physical touch, challenging defence mechanisms, and making interpretations. The given task, as requested by the school, was to help the group participants reflect on their mortality—an aim that, it is concluded, is not necessarily achievable or desirable.

The referral

The Special Educational Needs Co-ordinator (SENCO) of a local secondary school made a referral to our Clinic, requesting group therapy. He was worried about four children at the school who all had a terminal condition. He felt that the children would benefit from having some time with a therapist to think about their condition and "the future". All of the children and their parents had been asked whether they would like to be referred for a group, and all had agreed. We also learnt that the staff at the school were having difficulty in addressing the painful issues of illness and death while continuing to carry out their roles as teachers within the school, and therefore the decision had been made to refer to an outside agency. In our initial consultation with the school, it seemed that they were expecting a psycho-educational group to be set up in order to address issues of loss and bereavement. However, following our assessments with each of the proposed group members, it was clear that the intense nature of the children's anxiety warranted a less directive therapeutic group. It was felt to be most appropriate to provide a group drawing on ideas from psychodynamic and analytic group therapy.

Following a meeting with each of the children's parents, the group was set up to contain four children, all of whom had muscular dystrophy, some with associated learning disabilities. Of the four originally referred, two have left the group—one left the school and one was hospitalized long-term—and a girl with a musculo-skeletal disorder has joined. These children all had advanced progressive disease causing major difficulties with mobility and extensive, although uncertain, limitations to their life expectancy. Over the course of running this group, we have been aware of many dilemmas that have been generated by this work. This chapter explores some of the dilemmas and difficulties in working with a group of children with such specific difficulties—that is, of having physical disabilities, combined with either a shortened life expectancy or a terminal condition. In addition, all the children are in early adolescence and are struggling with the challenges this brings. Before we think about the group in detail, it would be helpful to describe the three children who are currently attending the group.

The children

"Andrew"

The first of these children is a 12-year-old boy, whom we shall call Andrew. When Andrew was born, it was clear that he had major physical disabilities. He was therefore in hospital at frequent intervals for the first six years of his life. Andrew now lives at home with his mother, father, and siblings. We have heard from Andrew's father that his mother is clinically depressed, and he believes that this is due to Andrew's illness. Andrew is in a very old, slow, motorized wheelchair, and he has virtually no independent movement other than in the tips of his fingers. His head is supported by a brace, and his chest heaves with the effort of breathing. Andrew finds it difficult to play, not only with toys, but also with thoughts and ideas. Andrew's verbal skills are one of his strengths, but we have found that he is reluctant to talk about himself or his feelings. This could be considered as an aspect of adolescence; however, it could also be viewed as a defence against the painful reality of facing his disability. We have wondered if his difficulty in playing is related to his early life, his many hospitalizations, and his mother's depression. Bion (1962a) has described the important function of the mother in providing the infant with her containing and thoughtful state of mind, so that when the infant projects uncomfortable, distressing feelings, the mother can process these feelings and return them in a more digestible form. One could hypothesize that Andrew's difficulty in imaginative play relates to his early experience when the adults around Andrew were not readily able to think about his distress, perhaps because of their own anxieties about his condition.

"Michael"

Michael is 13 years old and has serious physical disabilities. He also uses a wheelchair, with his head supported by a brace. It is a much newer, faster, and more efficient model than Andrew's. Michael's older brother, who also had muscular dystrophy, died at the age of 10, when Michael was 6 years old. Michael presents as a child who is able to play and to express his thoughts and feelings.

Although his family were having to deal with the deterioration in his brother's condition and his eventual death, Michael appears to have a sense that his anxieties and distress can be thought about, held, and contained. This ability is illustrated in some of the clinical examples we consider.

"Kelly"

Finally, Kelly is a 13-year-old girl who has a musculo-skeletal condition. She is very vocal and interested in her environment, but she has little independent movement. She is positioned horizontally in her wheelchair, and her muscles have wasted away with the lack of use. She lives at home with her mother but has regular contact with her father. Kelly shows much insight in talking about her feelings, and she often vocalizes distress and anger for the rest of the group; however, this can also isolate her. We are constantly made aware of an alliance between Michael and Andrew that excludes Kelly—possibly due to her gender and the fact that they have the same condition.

The setting

The group has a box of play equipment specifically selected for the children. It includes cars, animals, a number of small human figures, pens and paper. All the children have the ability to manipulate objects when their arms are held in a supportive position.

The group meets in a large room in the school. We negotiated with the head teacher the use of a non-teaching room on a regular basis. However, due to the busy and overcrowded nature of the school and, at times, poor communication, we experienced several changes in room and regular interruptions to the group. The current group room is rather exposed, with windows looking onto a playground area on two sides. It is, however, the third different room that we have used over the course of running the group.

There are difficulties in working within a school setting, and this brings us to the first dilemma: how to manage running a therapeutically orientated group within a such a setting. We are aware that in a busy school it is difficult to provide a space on a regular basis, but at times the interruptions we have experienced have become intrusive. We have tried to make sense of the difficulty on the school's part in allowing the group a regular and uninterrupted space. The head teacher and the staff group were supportive and eager for the group to take place, and we have wondered whether the difficulties that they, and the other children in the school, demonstrate in allowing space for this particular group lie at an unconscious level. The nature of the children's disabilities leads them to be a particularly time-consuming and demanding group. McCormack (1991) describes the process whereby when others, such as the other children at the school and the staff, feel deprived and excluded, envious feelings can become quite intense. It is important to note that the staff initially requested the group because they felt that the children all needed a space to think about their own mortality. We wondered how defensive this position might be—how unbearable it feels for staff members who work so closely with the children to have to think about the future. It seems to us that giving the space for the group eases the anxiety in those workers, and this inevitably leads to feelings of guilt in the school staff (such as thoughts like "I can't talk about it or bear it", "I am glad it is not me or my child"). Our experience of the inability to protect the group has been painful and frustrating. Our countertransference feelings are of helplessness and being at the whim of others, possibly reflecting the way the children in the group have few means by which they can prevent being moved and pushed around by others.

The importance of providing an adequate emotional, physical, and relational environment in order for development to take place has been thought about from many perspectives. We have already mentioned Bion's (1962a) work on containment. Winnicott (1960) describes the importance for development of providing a "holding environment", which has a slightly different function from Bion's ideas about containment. Winnicott focuses on the physical environment as well as emotional relationships. Bowlby (1979) emphasizes the importance of the early environment in his description of attachment theory. He describes how an infant needs to form a positive relationship with its main carer—in his words, "a secure base"—in order for development to occur.

In light of these issues, how could we provide the group with a containing environment in which thinking could be facilitated and nurtured? We have been struck by how concretely intrusions damage the developing thoughts in the group. An example of an early group session illustrates this:

> In this session, the group are finding ways to think about the future. Andrew has asked to make a fortune-teller: a structure made out of paper that is folded to cover various statements that aim to tell one's fortune. (The operator asks the participant for a series of numbers and manipulates the structure according to the numbers given; the final number is used to identify a flap in the structure, the flap corresponding to that number is opened, and the fortune is told.) Michael is interested in the process. Andrew cannot physically fold the paper, and step-by-step he instructs the therapist. Michael tells Andrew that he should put in "getting a girlfriend" and "winning lots of money". Andrew is less able to allow himself to fantasize about the future; he says he will put in "you smell", "you are good at football", and "I love you". We are aware of the importance of fantasies about the future, like the dreams and aspirations of non-disabled children. For our group, these fantasies help to bridge the gap between their reality and their ideal self, but they also provide a function of denial, defending against the dreadful anxiety about how long they actually have to live. It was felt that any comment drawing their attention to this defence would feel too threatening, so one therapist says that Michael and Andrew both have lots of ideas about what they want to put into the fortune-teller, and they may also be having thoughts about us, the therapists, and what our lives are like. The children are able to develop their ideas about what to put in. Michael says, "What about driving a fast car", and Andrew replies "Yeah, and flying a plane". At this point the door bursts open, and a girl comes in. We ask her to leave, saying clearly that it is a private group. Under their breath Michael, Andrew, and Kelly say, "Go away, Eesha." She says, "but I just want to get my crisps", and she quickly crosses the room. One of the therapists gets up to usher her out and closes the door firmly behind her. Kelly shouts at the door ". . . and don't come back".

Michael rudely tells Kelly to "shut up" as he can't concentrate with all the yelling, and Andrew seems remote and unreactive. The therapist comments on how angry the group feel about Eesha's intrusion. The therapists have thoughts about the impact on Andrew of the disturbance and how this relates to his early life in hospital. The children are no longer able to talk about the fortune-tellers; they want to discuss football instead. The therapist asks if they would like her to continue folding the paper. The children ignore her, and she comments on how cross they feel with her too, not being able to stop the interruption. She is made to feel some of the helplessness and frustration that is being experienced.

Drawing on our own feelings and our emotional responses to the group processes was vital in understanding the mechanisms at work in both the individuals and in the group as a whole. Reid (1999) notes that the use of countertransference becomes paramount when working with people who are unable to verbalize their feelings. In our view this was a group with particular difficulties in experiencing and expressing their feelings. In this example we are made aware of how hard it is to generate a good-enough sense of being held internally when the external holding environment is not quite good enough.

Nitsun (1989) has compared the development of a group with the development of an infant. The provision of a good-enough holding function is essential if the group is to be able to achieve any integration, just the way an infant needs containment in order to develop. It was incidents like the one described above that prompted us to go back to the SENCO who had requested the group and the other staff to think about ways in which the group could be protected. More recently we have been able to organize some times for the teaching staff to think about the process of the group, and this time for reflection has proved invaluable in terms of our relationship with the school. It could be hypothesized that thinking with the staff enabled them to feel held, and permission was then given for the group to be held in a more protected environment. We have learnt the importance of working with the organization in order to protect the group, at the risk that the children may feel their confidentiality is being broken. On reflection, the group would have benefited from some initial work with the staff to set a clear contract of expectations on both sides prior to the group starting.

The use of touch and its impact on the therapeutic process

The second dilemma we wanted to think about is that of physical contact. This arises from the fact that the children are totally dependant on us physically. If they want to draw, we must hold up their arms so that the nib of the pen can make contact with the paper. If they wish to look in a different direction, they ask us to undo their head brace, reposition their head, and redo the brace. Obviously we cannot predict what they want to do or see, so the need to make physical requests of us is never-ending. This creates dilemmas about how to manage the transference. The example of a group session that followed the Christmas break where all three children were together for the first time in several months illustrates this dilemma:

> At the beginning of the group, Michael made a request to leave the room to collect his table from another room. We have talked about the importance of not coming and going, and we tell him, no, that one of us will go and get the table. Michael is cross and he wants to leave, but he cannot switch his wheelchair on, so he is stuck. He says angrily that he hates us and he never wants to come back to the group again. One therapist leaves the room to collect the table, and Michael becomes angry with the other children for continuing with their activities and not supporting him. He shouts and swears at the therapist, and Kelly tries to calm him. Michael tells the therapist that he will destroy the contents of the group box when we are not looking. When the other therapist returns, Michael's anxiety is talked about; we comment on how there has been a break and that it doesn't feel okay that one of us has left the room even though he wanted his table. We did not make the group feel safe by one of us leaving and that he feels very angry—perhaps they all feel cross with us about the break, and all being here today does feel quite scary. Michael calms and is able to ask the therapist who left the room

to help him; however, he refuses to respond to the other therapist until the end of the group, when he finds it very difficult to leave. We comment on his fear that he has damaged us with his very powerful feelings and his fears that if he leaves, it will be difficult to come back, or that we will not allow him back in retaliation. Michael looks visibly relieved, and as he goes, he calls, "Good bye, see you next week."

Bion (1962a) describes the process whereby groups avoid the main group task by moving into a "group basic assumption". He describes the three basic assumption processes as "fight/flight", "pairing", and "dependence". Michael seemed to be trying to draw the group into a fight mentality; however, at this time the group is strong enough to resist this. Michael then resorts to splitting the two therapists: one into a threatening figure, the other into an idealized one. As Klein (1946) has suggested, Michael may be using splitting as a defence against the painful feelings about his dependence on others. In order to contain the anxiety provoked by his dependence, he has projected all the bad and difficult feelings into one therapist and idealized the other therapist as a way of protecting himself against these bad feelings. Michael is able to use the group to explore his anxieties in this way. It is by observing this type of behaviour in the group that we have become aware how difficult it is to use us in this way when the children are physically dependent on us for their every move.

The anxieties about physical contact are felt strongly by the children themselves. They are acutely aware of the physical nature of their relationships with all others, and the group is no exception. It raises oedipal feelings about the relationship between the two therapists and also about each therapist and their external life, partners, and possible children. The children in the group have a tendency to try to claim a therapist for themselves by making repeated demands on one therapist in particular, and this creates great anxiety and perceived threat when all three children are present and there are only two therapists. We are all confronted with the reality that there is just not enough to go around. These oedipal feelings are all the more difficult because the children are excluded not only from relationships but also from their own imagined future. This issue was highlighted in a painful session when Michael was the only child to attend a group session. The nature of their conditions means that all of the children miss some school and group time, but we do feel it is important to maintain the sessions as group therapy (rather than individual therapy), even when only one child is present.

In this session, Michael had brought in some photos taken over the recent holiday that he was keen for us to see. We looked at the photos: they were of his family—his mother, father, little sister, and visiting grandmother. We talked of how he wanted to share his home with us and to make a connection between home and the group. He told us that he wanted us to come to his home, and he asked us, quite hesitantly, if we would come to his birthday party in a few months. Birthdays to the children are so much more than a party: they are the survival of another year, month, day, and hour. As noted by Sinason (1992b), birthdays in the life of a person with a disability also represent a reminder of their creation, what went wrong in the process, and how people responded to their birth. As mentioned, Michael's older brother suffered from the same condition and had been diagnosed by the time Michael was born.

We gently tell Michael that he does really know that we won't be able to come to his party, but that this feels so hurtful. Michael asks for the photos to be put away, then asks for his Walkman to be put on, excluding both his thoughts and us. He fiddles with the Walkman for the rest of the session, but when we come to the end, he is reluctant to leave. As in the incident described previously, he is terrified of the damage his thoughts might cause. We comment on his anxiety about being cross with us and his fear that we, too, will be cross with him and how difficult it is to leave when there are such uncomfortable feelings around.

Defence mechanisms used in the group process

Evans (1998) notes that splitting, denial, and control are common defence mechanisms used by adolescents when observed in groups. In group therapy it is considered helpful for the therapist to point out what the young person is attempting to deny or dissociate from, in order to increase the individual's capacity for self-knowledge and to reduce their anxiety associated with the avoided topic. Over the duration of our group it has become increasingly difficult to know how best to question the defence mechanisms by this group and whether or not it is appropriate to challenge these defences. Altschuler (1997) comments that this dilemma is especially important when working with chronically ill children. Indeed, at times it can be very tempting to follow a model of supportive psychotherapy, to let the unconscious feelings remain unconscious and avoid the painful future that the children are facing. The aim of the group, however, was to provide a space for the children to explore their thoughts and feelings about the progressive illnesses that they are suffering from, about disabilities, and about dying.

Splitting and projection

Defence mechanisms of splitting and projection can help to protect a child from the pain of illness or disability but as a result may prevent effective mourning of the loss of ability or health and lead to psychological distress.

Michael is often the child who verbally offers the group an opportunity to talk about death. However, he demonstrates strong defence mechanisms of splitting and projection to protect himself when the thoughts become unbearable.

> In a session where Andrew has been absent for several weeks, Michael asks the group to guess who gave him his pencil case. After several wrong guesses Michael says that he has had it for a long time, and the person who gave it to him had a name that begins with "J". Kelly immediately guesses that the case was from Michael's brother. One of the therapists asks Michael his

brother's name; he says, "John. He's dead, he had the same problem as me." Michael is keen for Kelly to remember his brother, telling her that he had attended the same school, and she had met him. The therapist says she feels it is hard to think about John and that Michael wants him to be remembered by the group. The therapist comments that the children may also be thinking about Andrew, who has been away from the group for four weeks. Michael says, " Andrew won't live long; he is very sick." Kelly agrees and says that she is very worried about Andrew. Michael tells of how he knows Andrew has been using oxygen to help him breathe. The therapist comments that it is very frightening to think about people close to you being so ill that they might not live. Michael says they are close "like brothers—blood brothers" and then quickly changes the subject, asking for help with his fountain pen. The therapist comments on the change of subject and uses the term "blood brothers" in her interpretation. Michael becomes angry and says, "Don't use that word, I hate it." We wonder out loud if it was difficult to think about these painful things. Michael's response is to say that Kelly is very upset and is trying not to cry. Kelly denies this, and the children start to talk about the difficulties they have with their teachers.

This example clearly illustrates Michael using defences against the pain of thinking about his own and his friend's condition.

Denial

The strongest defensive position is denial, and this is an important mechanism that the group has developed to defend against the extreme anxiety that their illnesses and prognoses evoke. This is clearly illustrated in an example from the group. Michael had been absent from the group for two consecutive sessions due to illness.

In the first of these sessions Kelly starts to talk about Michael in an idealized way, saying he is big and great and how everyone looks up to him. Kelly talks about how she thinks everyone talks down to her and treats her like a child, but this would never happen to Michael. She goes on to say that when Michael grows up, he will drive a fast car and will get all the girls and that she and Andrew will just end up being his servants. Andrew agrees and says that he and Kelly need to stick together like best buddies. In the next session, when one of the therapists comments on Michael's continued absence, Andrew immediately picks up the conversation from the previous session, saying that he thinks Michael will be a pop star, a millionaire, will drive two Ferraris and have loads of girlfriends. The therapist wonders if the children are worried about Michael being absent from the group and if they do not want to think about what might be wrong with him, they prefer to think about him as independent, successful, and having a great time. The children immediately change the subject and talk about how angry they feel with their teachers and what they don't like about school. The thought of what might be happening to Michael is unbearable; the sad and guilty feelings that these thoughts evoke are immediately turned into angry feelings directed against school, teachers, and therapists who are unable to meet their needs. It feels more comfortable to be engrossed in a fight than suddenly to wonder what the fight is about and be faced with sadness instead of anger.

Interventions that use interpretation of defences as a means to develop deeper understanding of unconscious processes at play need to accommodate the reality of the child's experiences, and therapists need to modify their style accordingly. Emanuel (1990) urges the need for caution owing to what he describes as the catastrophic anxiety that may lie behind these defences. He advocates that the protective nature of these defences should be respected and not challenged too harshly. In any group there is also the aim of allowing space and time for the members to think about themselves as individuals in relation to the group. The example illustrates the difficulty the children face in relation to their own prognosis and how this is translated into a painful reality by witnessing the physical deterioration of the fellow group members.

Strong defences, however, can become a barrier to learning, both about oneself and in a scholastic sense. McCormack (1991) notes that in order to learn, one must be directed towards certain tasks. In order to be curious, one must have a memory, and one must be able to think. When faced with disability at such a concrete level as this group of children, it is difficult to see how learning cannot be impaired. If the child is unable to bear thoughts or tolerate frustration, then thinking will be severely impaired. It is important to note that all three children have been diagnosed as having mild learning disabilities.

Andrew finds it very difficult to draw, but when his arm is supported, he can both write and draw. On one occasion he strained very hard throughout a whole group to produce a picture of fireworks on black paper. The children were talking about how they couldn't get to see the fireworks because of their wheelchairs. As we neared the end of the group, Andrew realized that he could not finish his picture, and he was very unhappy with it, saying that it didn't even look like fireworks, it was rubbish and a waste of time. He pushed it to the floor and insisted that the drawing was thrown away. This example demonstrates how the children frequently destroy any achievements and how painful the reality is when things are not perfect. This brought to mind Sinason's (1992b) valuable ideas regarding "secondary handicap"—that is, exaggerating one's difficulties as a way of defending against the pain of the actual disability. Sinason maintains that secondary handicap is in itself a barrier to learning.

The dilemma of making interpretations

Linked to the dilemma of challenging defence mechanisms are our thoughts about the usefulness of interpretations. Rycroft (1968) defines correct interpretations as "those which explain the material and are formulated in such a way and communicated at such a time that they make sense to the patient". They aim to "increase self-awareness and therefore facilitate integration by making the person conscious of the processes within himself that were previously unconscious". As mentioned earlier, Bion's (1961) work on group processes has helped us to think about this particular group. Bion states that the group facilitator should focus on "group-as-a-whole" interpretations as opposed to making separate therapeutic interpretations to individuals within the group. As we have described above, each member of the group is using different defences and is at a different level of acceptance in relation to their condition. While this is to be expected, it does create a dilemma about the level at which our comments and interpretations should be aimed. Michael's anxiety is often modified when we have made comments about the levels of anger in the group, while Andrew's anxiety seems to increase at these times. We appreciate that this is a group process and the group are working through a particular task, at this time about managing anger, but any therapeutic comment needs to be considered very carefully, given the potential for increasing catastrophic anxiety. We relied heavily on our countertransference feelings to decide whether an interpretation was helpful or necessary. Given the fragility of the children's psychological states, if we felt any doubt, we considered it more appropriate not to make an interpretation.

Discussion

It is our belief that children who have advanced progressive disease that severely limits their mobility and results in an extensive though uncertain curtailment in life expectancy presents group therapists with an unusual and difficult task. McCormack (1991) talks about the use of psychotherapy with people with disabilities in order to develop a discourse around a person's history, denied because of the pain of bearing the individual's handicap.

In bearing the person's past experience, we believe that we should be able to construct a positive future, to the extent that this is possible, in the face of the reality of their increasing disability and eventual death. From our experience the extent to which our group members could bear their painful reality was severely limited, and an open discussion of this was further inhibited by their considerable concern for others', including their therapists', sensibilities and awareness of their problems. We do not believe that an open discussion of mortality was an achievable task. However, despite the powerful defences that all the children demonstrated, we are very conscious of how important it was for ourselves as therapists to be aware of these facts and to be able to bear the children's distress, even though we did not articulate this openly. Our comments to the group needed to be judged with considerable caution based upon our intuitive sense of the children's individual and collective states of mind. Through this necessarily delicate and difficult process we believe that these children were helped, in terms both of their feelings about their condition and of its impact on their adolescence.

It is our belief that children with the types of difficulties described above present the group therapist with an unusual task. McCormack (1991) talks about the use of psychotherapy with people with disabilities to develop a discourse around a person's history, denied because of the pain of bearing the individual's handicap. In bearing the person's past experience, we should also be freer to construct a positive future in the face of the unbearable truth of increasing disability and eventual death. However, for the patient this also means managing the transference and countertransference feelings while maintaining a physically dependent relationship with the therapist. This is a real focus of the work for the children: how to allow themselves to think about their anxieties while protecting the therapists from their very powerful negative feelings. This is a fine line to tread, and the work is therefore necessarily slow. The requested task of focusing on mortality is not, in our opinion, an achievable aim. The children have all demonstrated their need to protect themselves against a truly dreadful reality, which needs to be respected. However, if we are not able to bear the children's unbearable thoughts and feelings, we leave them vulnerable to deeper distress and anxiety.

We are unable, for lack of space, to describe some of the other constant themes that arose in this group, such as dealing with gender issues, sexuality, culture, and religion. Not surprisingly, a major focus of the group has been that of negotiating the tasks of adolescence: although they are physically and learning-disabled children, they are, first and foremost, children.

CHAPTER THREE

Some thoughts on psychotherapeutic work with learning-disabled children and their parents from orthodox religious communities

Judith Usiskin

This chapter describes therapeutic work with patients from orthodox religious communities of several faiths—Muslim, Jewish, and Fundamentalist Christian—that had, as a common factor, that all the children had various degrees of learning disability. The constraints imposed on the therapist in terms of some of the issues that arose in therapy with this client group are explored, as well as the impact of the learning disabilities factor on family dynamics, including cultural attitudes towards handicap.

In order to preserve confidentiality, all personal data have been changed, and, where necessary, the clinical material has been disguised to make the patients unidentifiable. This has not been an easy task, as all the patients described are, of course, very special individuals, with their own particular traits, mores, and family backgrounds; I hope that despite this rather rigorous editing I have been able to capture their individuality and to convey their particular needs.

Organizations like NAFSIYAT (the Inter-cultural Therapy Centre) have been working therapeutically with patients from a variety of ethnic backgrounds for many years. The most recent publications by professionals working in this Clinic—such as Renos

Papadopoulos (2001, 2002), Gill Gorell-Barnes (2002), and Inga-Britt Krause (2002), to name but a few—have provided us with further insight and understanding in this area of work. The Tavistock Clinic Bangladeshi Service has been in force since 1996, providing consultation and treatment for members of the Bangladeshi community.

This chapter explores some of the difficulties in working psychotherapeutically with culturally diverse patients and issues such as the absence of shared language, hierarchical structures, social ranking, and the meaning of gestures such as touch or eye contact are addressed; the main focus, however, is on the particular impact orthodox religion has had on the therapeutic work with this group of learning-disabled patients.

The first chapter of the Old Testament, Genesis, refers to Chaos and Abyss, when land and sea cannot be differentiated. Discovering that a child is born with a disability can create similar chaos and confusion in the parent's mind. The child expected is not the child born—the narcissistic injury that has taken place is hard to manage for most parents. Instead of the normal, healthy baby looked forward to, a child is born which does not conform to their expectations. Fears that were harboured in the farthest corner of a parent's mind and often not expressed at a conscious level have become reality.

Once the child is born, in some cases parents may blame each other for this misfortune, if, indeed, they experience it as such. Doctors, nurses, or midwives may be blamed, and the parents themselves may experience intense feelings of guilt.

One mother whom I interviewed as part of a research project (Bichard, Sinason, & Usiskin, 1996) said to me: "I knew something was wrong all along, as soon as he was born, and I tried to tell the doctors, but they said I was a fusspot, that he [her son] was just a little behind because he had been born prematurely. But I knew he was not normal, and he turned out to be severely handicapped, and he developed mental-health problems on top of it all. But maybe it was God's punishment, me being unhappy in my marriage and all that."

I have been working as a Child and Adolescent Psychotherapist for over ten years now and have had experience in working therapeutically with patients with learning disabilities for more than twenty years. Nevertheless, it is only in the last couple of years that I have become involved in working psycho-dynamically with young people and families from orthodox religious backgrounds. As an agnostic with no religious upbringing, it had never been a burning interest of mine to explore the subject of religion, and I had little conscious experience of therapeutic work with this group of patients. My experience of having visited synagogues, churches, and occasionally a mosque was limited to weddings, christenings, and funerals, and although I was able to appreciate the service itself, the music (if that was part of it), and the containing function that such rituals no doubt fulfil, I remained an outsider.

Between 1999 and 2001, our Service received several referrals of children from orthodox religious communities, and I decided to undertake a small number of assessments. The children spanned an age range between 2 and 16, both male and female.

To give you a flavour of the work, I have selected three cases; I describe the assessments and then move on to treatment and the particular issues that arose, both for the patients and myself.

Assessment 1: "Rebeccah", aged 3

My first assessment encounter was with the mother of a severely handicapped little girl, whom I have called Rebeccah, and her brother "Rafi", two years older, who also had global developmental delays. The children's problems were congenital.

Their mother, Mrs X, originally from a secular Jewish background, had become attracted to the more orthodox religious beliefs and customs of Judaism in her late teens during a gap year spent in Israel, and several years later she had cemented her change of heart by marrying an orthodox Israeli.

The referred patient was Rebeccah, Mrs X's second child, but the GP had requested an assessment of the whole family, because mother had developed depression following the birth of her daughter, Rebeccah, who was diagnosed with a condition similar to that of her son, Rafi.

Mr and Mrs X were invited to the first appointment together, without the children, but Mr X did not attend. Instead, Mrs X came with both the children. She was wearing a wig, a traditional custom among orthodox women.

I introduced myself, and she responded in a rather depressed, flat manner. I acknowledged her husband not being present, and Mrs X explained that he felt he was being labelled by coming to an establishment such as this Clinic. Mrs X seemed somewhat resigned that she had been left to "go it alone", as it were, and she looked sad.

We were able to talk about some of the difficulties having two handicapped children presented, and Mrs X told me that her husband's family were blaming her for this, as well as seeing it as their son's punishment for having married someone from a non-orthodox background. Mrs X described her husband as being less conscientious in terms of fulfilling his religious duties than she was, saying she felt she was taking the teachings, rules, and laws more seriously. I acknowledged that Mrs X had made a conscious choice to live according to a particularly strict set of beliefs rather than having been born into that culture, and she agreed that this might be an important factor in how the couple approached their faith.

Mrs X also told me that her own family had been against the marriage, but that they had already more or less cut off ties once she decided to adopt a religious way of life. In thinking with Mrs X about her difficulties, we made some links between what her parents perceived as the loss of their daughter as she had been, and her own experiences of the loss of her imagined two healthy, normal children.

During our first meeting the older child, Rafi, was slumped in his pushchair, looking like a doll, his head lolling from side to side. He was dressed in clothes that were slightly too big, and he looked a little unkempt. In contrast little Rebeccah, whose dark-brown eyes were staring straight ahead, was dressed in a pretty frock, dark ringlets framing her face and eyes. Mrs X had brought no toys for either of the children, and when I suggested I could provide some, she shook her head in a resigned kind of manner, saying "they don't know how to play". From her bag she produced a bottle of milk for Rebeccah and, putting it into her mouth, propped it up with a blanket. Rebeccah sucked listlessly, and Mrs X talked in a slow, somewhat laboured manner, complaining about the fact that she was unable to attend religious services as often as she wanted to as she had no one to look after the children. I acknowledged Mrs X's difficulties, and she seemed pleased to have been listened to. Rebeccah had stopped feeding, the bottle had dropped from her mouth, and she had dozed off. It was time to end the session, and when I confirmed with Mrs X that she would return the following week, she said she would be glad to.

Assessment 2: "Fuad", aged 8

The family's GP had referred Fuad, a boy from a Muslim background, because the Health Visitor had observed some unusual behaviours while attending the home after the birth of Fuad's youngest brother. She had subsequently expressed her concerns to the GP, suggesting that Fuad might be suffering from some psychological problems. Fuad was one of 12 children in his family—"somewhere in the middle", as he described himself during the assessment.

I met with Fuad on two occasions to assess his suitability for psychotherapy, and both meetings were remarkable. Fuad attended on time, brought by his father, but he was shy to enter the consulting-room. Being alone with a woman other than his mother or female family members might have played a part in it, and the unfamiliarity of the surroundings may also have contributed to his unease. He spoke in a whisper, making it difficult for me to hear what he was saying and forcing me to lean towards him.

I had provided the usual set of toys, including drawing materials, for Fuad, and it was the medium of drawing that eventually broke the ice. He took out the pens and paper and began drawing. His first picture was a map—a street map of where he lived, in South London, giving details including landmarks such as his local newsagents, parks, the public library, and the local supermarket, as well as his school, his siblings' schools, and the local mosque. I acknowledged that Fuad wanted me to know about the kind of surroundings familiar to him and said that perhaps he was also expressing an anxiety about coming to a new, strange place such as this Clinic. A big smile appeared on Fuad's face, and taking up pens and paper again, he continued to draw. His next picture was of a railway station, a busy thoroughfare that included porters, taxis, and buses. Fuad said he loved trains, and he had visited a lot of family members in the Midlands. Trains became an important feature in the subsequent therapy, standing for change generally as well as representing the particular changes in his life for which he longed. Fuad had a rather unrealistic picture in his mind, wanting to move to his family's country of origin and live there with his extended family. Because of his learning difficulties, Fuad experienced himself as burden to his family—as "I'm odd one out", in his words.

He compensated for his learning difficulties by having developed a remarkable capacity to memorize information, even though some of the time the meaning of things eluded him.

In our first meeting, with my encouragement, he also drew up his family tree, and this shed helpful light on his position in the family, as well as providing information about his older, grown-up siblings and their families.

Fuad was less anxious during our second meeting, and his confidence increased when I acknowledged that perhaps he had things to tell me from which I could learn, to do with his religious customs, the language spoken at home, the kinds of food he was able to eat, and the tasks he was expected to perform at school and within his religious community.

His parents were in agreement with Fuad being seen in therapy, albeit a little reluctant at first, and a Muslim colleague agreed to support the therapeutic work by meeting with them on a regular basis. This proved to be immensely helpful for all concerned.

Assessment 3: "Ian", aged 10

This describes work carried out at a unit other than the Tavistock, in a supervisory capacity. A request was received from Social Services to assess a young boy from a Christian fundamentalist background, who had been referred because of having sexually abused one of his younger male siblings. He was also experiencing difficulties at school, lacking concentration, and a psychological assessment had revealed mild learning difficulties. It was not clear whether his learning difficulties were due to trauma or to organic causes. Ian and his family, consisting of nine children, had moved to England because of legislation having been introduced in their home country that forbade corporal punishment being meted out by parents. The parents felt that physical chastisement was an important part of the children's upbringing, and they had acted on this belief continuously, administering regular beatings to all their children, both male and female. Corporal punishment has traditionally been part of disciplining children in the care of religious orders, and it is only recently that survivors of such abuse have dared to speak out and, in some cases, are suing their former abusers. An article by Beatrix Campbell (2003) in *The Guardian* newspaper highlighted the plight of a number of men and women—former residents of Nazareth House, an orphanage in Scotland—where they were physically, and in some cases, sexually abused by the nuns and by outsiders whose role it was to "befriend" the children.

Following the disclosures of physical and sexual abuse, Ian and his siblings were removed from their parents and placed under a full care order. Ian commenced psychotherapy once a stable foster placement had been identified.

During his assessment it was noted that Ian was unable to use any of the toys, saying he was not allowed to play, and despite much encouragement from his therapist, Ms B, he said he could not draw. He seemed afraid in the room, displaying frozen watchfulness. When Ms B unexpectedly moved her hand to adjust a comb that threatened to fall out of her hair, Ian flinched. He was able to acknowledge that he had been afraid of Ms B hitting him, and it became clear that the beatings he had received in the past were often unpredictable and administered randomly.

Ian displayed what Sinason (1992b) describes as "the handicapped smile". His face contorted into a broad grin, and what came to Ms B's mind was that Ian had been "grinning and bearing" the experiences from his abusive past. When this was acknowledged during his assessment, Ian was able to say that his father and mother had told him that it was important to look happy, "because of being one of God's chosen children".

Treatment

"Rebeccah" and the X family

Let us now return to Mrs X and her two handicapped children. Mrs X continued to attend on a regular basis, making good use of the sessions offered to her. Her husband never attended, but although this was a source of great disappointment to her, it gradually freed her up to talk about issues she said she felt uncomfortable discussing with him. Their sexual relationship presented concerns, in that sexual pleasure seemed to be considered an unacceptable part of sexual congress, the enjoyment making Mrs X feel both guilty and, in her own words, frivolous. Although having had permission to use contraception, this did not, however, in their minds, release them from the feelings of guilt that "spilling their seed in vain"—in other words having sexual intercourse without producing further children—evoked in them.

Further difficulties arose when Mr X went on a trip to America, leaving his wife behind to cope with the two children, making her feel lonely and abandoned. She harboured a suspicion that her husband was planning to divorce her and that he was having contact with a woman whom she suspected of having been the one originally chosen to marry him. Mrs X felt persecuted and accused Mr X's family of plotting against her and the children, and it took a great deal of time to help Mrs X understand that the feelings of inadequacy she was experiencing might in some ways be linked to her inability to make things better for her children.

When her husband eventually returned from his travels, she was able to confront him with her doubts, and it was at this stage that Mr X decided to attend a one-off meeting at the Clinic. This was experienced by all concerned as a major event. Mrs X felt both pleased that her husband had decided to come, but also worried at having to share her space. I felt curious and wondered whether the fantasies I had had bore any resemblance to the real Mr X.

Mr X presented as a tall, handsome young man of distinct Semitic appearance, with a beard and long side curls, dressed in black trousers, a white shirt, and a long black overcoat and wearing a skullcap. Mr X seemed to feel he had to make up for lost time, as he talked through most of the meeting. Questions directed at them as a couple were answered by Mr X, but Mrs X showed no sign of minding this. Her husband seemed to act as a kind of buffer between herself and me. This took me by surprise but also gave me an idea of how they might present as a couple to the outside world. Mr X decided to attend further sessions, and this considerably changed the dynamics of my work with Mrs X and the children. From then on, Mrs X took a back seat, letting her husband do most of the talking, and she clearly appreciated her husband's protective manner. Mr X rarely made eye contact with me during the meetings, looking at his wife while talking to me.

Initially discussions focused entirely on the difficulties they were experiencing with the children, but eventually a somewhat competitive scenario evolved in the sessions on the subject of domesticity, relating in particular to the preparation of the traditional foods reserved for Shabbat and holy days. Mr X seemed somewhat critical of his wife's ability to prepare the food stuffs in just the "right" way, and he had brought in a number of his female relatives to show his wife "how it's done". Mrs X perceived this as an insult, saying she was perfectly able to cook the food as it was meant to be prepared.

Mr X described family meals in great detail and lamented the fact that his children were not able to partake in these meals in an active way, which would have included reciting prayers and blessings. It felt as though some of his complaints about his wife's inability to cook the food in just the kind of way he was used to was in fact also a projection of his feelings of impotence where his children were concerned.

Food continued to be an issue during our meetings together, and often Mrs X fed the children in the sessions. The food she brought was always home-made and puréed, and she was keen to stress that it was very healthy.

Mr X raised issues to do with the kind of mental food his children needed to develop intellectually, saying he was concerned that their son would never be able to attend religious school but would have to go to a school for children with learning disabilities. Clearly this was a likely possibility, and Mr X found it particularly hard to acknowledge that his son, because of his difficulties, might not be able to fulfil his role in the religious community, let alone get married or have a family.

After a few weeks Mr X suddenly decided not to attend further sessions, and the reason given was because of work commitments. (He had a job teaching in a school for orthodox boys.) Mrs X continued to attend her appointments with the children, and as time went on they became more lively and, having become used to the setting, began to play with the toys provided. Rafi in particular played with the toy animals, and he seemed especially to like the toy lion and tiger, as well as the crocodile.

Despite the children being non-verbal, they managed to convey some of their feelings clearly through play and by making the appropriate noises when they were bored, sad, or frustrated. Together we thought about the meaning of their communications, and for Mrs X this became a useful tool for better understanding their emotional needs.

One day, after several months of work, I had a telephone call from Mrs X, telling me that her husband had gone to Israel with Rafi to visit his family, and, while there, they had been involved in an accident. Apparently Rafi had sustained some head injuries and was in hospital in Jerusalem. Mrs X decided to leave Rebeccah with one of her sisters-in-law and went to see her son. They returned to England after about one month, and the prognosis for Rafi was said to be worrying. He was admitted to hospital to be closely monitored for any changes.

Mrs X returned to the Clinic, and I found her to be guilt-ridden, saying she thought the accident was God's way of punishing her for having doubted her husband's commitment to her and the children.

* * *

Work with Mrs X continues to date, and there have been slight improvements in Rafi's condition.

"Fuad"

Fuad's therapy went extremely well: he was engaged in the work, and his main way of communicating remained the medium of drawing. A large collection of pictures emerged, functioning as a kind of historical commentary of the therapy. Fuad often referred to issues that had arisen with the help of his drawings. Psychically, I became the canvas for his projections—a mother who was sometimes scolded for not possessing enough knowledge of the intricacies of religious life, standing for his learning difficulties, and sometimes admired for interpreting his internal world, an area previously known only to Fuad himself. Most of all, an air of bemusement persisted as to who I was, what I represented, and the way in which I was different from the other women in his life.

As with Mrs X, food played a significant part in Fuad's culture, and I often heard about elaborate meals being prepared for festivals and high holidays. This information was sometimes aimed at provoking a sense of envy in me as well as reminding me of the symbolic function of food, standing for warmth and containment.

Following the events of 11 September, a sense of fear and mistrust began to manifest itself in the sessions with Fuad. Endless repetition of drawings depicting the fall of the twin towers ensued, as Fuad was trying to gauge my feelings and opinions on this issue by presenting me, through his drawings, with alternative versions of the event.

However, eventually the trust that had existed was re-established, and the therapeutic work continued for another year.

Fuad's therapy terminated after two and a half years, and much had been achieved. He had become more confident generally, and his parents reported that he had "found his voice within the family". Fuad received a Statement of Special Needs, and this enabled him to access the extra help needed in school.

"Ian"

At the beginning of therapy Ian presented as a troubled, mistrustful, undernourished-looking boy who avoided all eye contact. He looked neglected and had poor eyesight and poor hearing. His English was reasonably good, but his extreme anxiety initially seemed to inhibit any meaningful communication with his therapist.

Ian told Ms B that he and his brothers and sisters had felt lonely and isolated when coming to England and said they were teased at the school they attended, partly because of their accent, but also because of their unkempt looks and their old-fashioned style of dressing.

In treatment it became clear what a harsh, cruel, and punishing paternal object Ian had come to internalize during his life. In retaliation, male figures were being thrown off imaginary cliffs, burnt to death, or eaten by wild animals, or, in turn, they hit, kicked, and abused younger, weaker animals or toy people. Ms B herself was not immune from such abuse, and when angry, Ian often lashed out or tried to kick her. He invented scenarios in the room that mirrored his life experiences, such as trying to force the child dolls to memorize great chunks of biblical material and ridiculing and punishing them for their inability to repeat things.

Via the foster parents, Ms B heard that Ian was inflicting similar punishments on his classmates, and that a small gang who simultaneously both admired and detested him had formed around him. There was talk of exclusion, but the therapist working with the foster parents was able to offer consultation to staff members at the school to help facilitate a more understanding approach to Ian's complex needs.

As time went on, Ian's foster parents reported slight improvements. Ian was able to relax sometimes, and he began to join in some of the activities his older foster siblings were engaged in, such as playing games, doing sports, and watching television. The only activity allowed in his parental home had been the study of the scriptures.

Gradually Ian's hard protective shell began to soften, and Ms B was able to catch glimpses of a developing sense of self emerging from the constrictive, oppressive world that had gripped him for so long. One day Ian took genuine delight in the blossoms outside the window of the consulting-room, and he spoke of a neighbour's child suffering taunts from other children in the neighbourhood because she had a physical disability. Ian's rigid judgemental thinking also decreased somewhat, and as well as being able to express his anger when Ms B had to have time off work because of illness, he also showed empathy with her predicament.

Ian kept reverting back to being more aggressive and intolerant after contact visits with his parents, which, for inexplicable reasons, were not supervised. The therapist supporting the foster parents eventually contacted Ian's social worker, and in time the local authority managed to change the arrangements to supervised contact. This had a positive effect on Ian, and his episodes of calmness increased. Equally, the school reported that his level of concentration increased, and he made progress academically. Peer relationships remained difficult, however, and Ian's capacity to tolerate children being cheeky or misbehaving was limited. He called them "stupid" and delighted in watching his peers being told off and often snitched on them in order to get them into trouble.

After approximately six months of treatment, an interesting development surfaced in the therapy-room. Ian took a particular interest in one of the toys in his box—a plastic dinosaur. He seemed fascinated by its looks and kept saying that it was no ordinary animal. This brought up the question of evolution, a subject completely unknown to Ian. When Ms B talked about this concept, she was met with disbelief and downright contempt. Did she not know that God had created the world in seven days? She must be stupid, then. Ms B suddenly found herself confronted with what she described as a brick wall, with no further thinking allowed to penetrate. Ian's hostility returned, and he pretended not to understand Ms B's comments and interpretations and ridiculed her for not speaking his mother tongue. It seemed that being confronted with new perspectives on the world was experienced as very threatening and led Ian to protect himself by making use of what Sinason called "opportunist handicap" (Sinason, 1992b). This is defined as a person with a learning disability using their handicap as a means to an end. Ian, being faced with information he felt to be threatening and difficult to process, sought refuge by deliberately not understanding.

Ian continued to see Ms B, and she was able to increase Ian's sessions to twice weekly, with positive effect. Gradually a boy with a more robust ego began to emerge, who was able to tolerate both praise and criticism and who, through therapy, had managed to internalize a solid, reliable maternal object in the form of his therapist. Although still struggling at school academically, his relationships improved, and he gained the trust of his peers.

Discussion

Freud, in his seminal work *Civilisation and Its Discontents* comments on the origins of religion:

> To me the derivation of religious needs from the helplessness of the child and a longing for its father seems irrefutable, especially as this feeling is not only prolonged from the days of childhood, but constantly sustained by a fear of the superior power of fate. I cannot cite any childish need that is as strong as the need for paternal protection. The role of the oceanic feeling, which might seek to restore unlimited narcissism, is thus pushed out of the foreground. The origin of the religious temperament can be traced in clear outline to the child's feeling of helplessness. [Freud, 1930a]

The work with Mrs X, Fuad's therapy, as well as Ms B's work with Ian all illustrate how great a part religion played in these patients' lives, both at an external and an internal level.

Ian's experiences of a misguided, abusive approach to religion damaged him considerably, and if we take Freud's notion of the child's longing for paternal protection based on feelings of helplessness, Ian's problems come as no surprise. His need to control was paramount, and he was able to convey to Ms B what it was like to be at the receiving end of it, making her feel as though she were suffocating during some of the sessions. Ian's parents had literally "drummed" their rigid morality into the children, turning them into frightened, terrified beings whose only way was to re-enact their experiences by inflicting them on others.

In contrast, Fuad was able in his sessions to draw on his religious background in a way that was both helpful and enriching. His confidence increased, and he was proud to talk about rules and rituals, such as dietary laws, as well as customs and festivities. Food played an important role, both at a practical and a symbolic level, whereas the absence of any such material in Ian's therapy was noted. Starved both emotionally and physically, Ian had come to accept the lack of proper, nourishing food as normal.

When Fuad began treatment, I noted that he often looked at the clothes I wore with great interest. His mother was covered from head to toe, including wearing a yashmak that left only her eyes visible. I found myself becoming aware of the clothes I chose to wear on the days of Fuad's therapy, particularly at the height of summer. In the therapy-room seating arrangements became an issue, as in order to hear what he was saying, I had to be close to him. Once his voice became stronger, I made some changes that allowed us to sit farther apart. Occasionally Fuad expressed surprise when I asked for clarification of something he was trying to communicate, yet inevitably he proceeded to explain with great zeal and patience, including teaching me words in Arabic.

I would like to focus briefly on some the issues that arose during the work with Mr and Mrs X and their children. For this family the children's disabilities were most worrying. It seemed as though neither parent had in any way come to terms with the shock of having two handicapped children. They seemed to share an unconscious phantasy that "bad sex" had damaged the children, although of course at a conscious level both parents were aware of the medical diagnoses.

The cessation of any meaningful contact with her own family was another painful issue. In the transference I sometimes stood for the mother who had abandoned her, who could not make things better for her, and at other times I was idealized. Mrs X, having chosen to become orthodox, was most concerned with fulfilling her religious duties according to the rules, and her sincerity was striking and impressive, leaving me feeling envious at times.

The experience of working with this group of patients has been rewarding and enriching. The work has allowed me insight into the meaning of group identity, the demands religious orthodoxy makes on its followers, the containment that "belonging" can provide, as well as catching a glimpse of what happens when religion is misinterpreted, leading to abuse.

CHAPTER FOUR

Facing the damage together: some reflections arising from the treatment in psychotherapy of a severely mentally handicapped child

Louise Emanuel

In Shakespeare's play *Richard III*, the Duchess of York, his mother, complains resentfully:

Thou cam'st on earth to make the earth my hell.
A grievous burden was thy birth to me.
Tetchy and wayward was thy infancy;
Thy school-days frightful, desperate, wild and furious;
                    [*Richard III*, IV.iv.167–170]

I am sure we can recognize this as a common description of the early life of patients we see in therapy, where there has been a mismatch or failure of attachment between mother and infant. Parents may feel for a range of reasons that their children are unlovable or incapable of giving pleasure, often projecting these feelings into their infants. Richard's parents lived in violent,

---

This chapter previously appeared in the *Journal of Child Psychotherapy*, 23 (1997, no. 2): 279–302. The Journal's website can be found at <www.tandf.co.uk>.

This work was written up some time ago when the term "mental handicap" was commonly used. It is unusual to use this today, and the term "learning disability" has become standard practice.

bloody times; his mother must have been more-or-less a single parent while her husband, the Duke of York, fought bitterly to attain the crown. However, I wonder whether Richard's congenital deformity played a part in her hatred of him. One can imagine her shock, feelings of failure, and outrage on discovering that she had given birth to a deformed child. She almost implies that he was sent to punish her for her sins. The beautiful, loveable baby that may have been there in phantasy for his parents was absent at his birth, had in a sense "died" and was replaced by a damaged baby. The difficult process of mourning the loss of one baby while attempting to welcome another, different baby would need to take place. I think this is a task that is seldom adequately done, and a failure to mourn the loss brings into focus all the attendant difficulties described so clearly by Freud (1917e) and Klein (1940). Richard's initial handicap, his physical deformity, may have been compounded by secondary emotional damage suffered as a result of his parents' inadequate mourning.

As I hear about an increasing number of handicapped children and the kinds of disturbed emotional behaviour many of them display, I am beginning to think that an early disturbance in the relationship between mother and infant from birth is almost inevitable. Feelings of grief and anger in parents, when faced with a damaged baby, are seldom processed. The unbearable fact of damage cannot be thought about and thereby contained, and projections into the baby of disappointment, or even horror, can take place. As a result, these children often grow up having internalized a disappointed, rejecting, even horrified object, and they may feel unworthy of love and deserving of rejection. The "primary handicap"—initial disability—can be compounded by the development of a "secondary handicap" (Sinason, 1992a, 1992c) through projective identification with this disappointed internal object. The infant attempts to refuse entry to these damaging projections by, for example, adopting autistic-type states of withdrawal or developing feeding difficulties. Alternatively, she may develop disruptive, challenging behaviour as she redoubles her attempts to project her feelings into an unreceptive, possibly depressed mother.

An extreme lack of containment of the infant's primitive communications, in turn, affects the infant's capacity to internalize a containing object and develop a mind to think (Bion, 1967a). In some cases a severe impairment in the capacity to think can lead to assumptions of more extensive organic damage than there may actually be.

For the reasons suggested above, I think it is very difficult for a "normal" attachment to develop between a mother and her damaged baby. Donald Meltzer adds another dimension to this idea by linking a failure of emotional bonding between mother and her damaged infant to the aesthetic impact they make on each other. In this chapter I develop these ideas and try to illustrate them with material from the treatment in psychotherapy of a severely mentally handicapped child whom I saw for 14 months on her own and then together with her father and younger brothers. I also raise some technical and ethical issues with which I was faced in dealing with such a profoundly damaged child.

"Primary disappointment" and "aesthetic reciprocity"

Ricky Emanuel has written about the baby's "primary disappointment" when his innate expectation of containment by an object is not realized (Emanuel, 1984). I think the mother of a child born handicapped has a converse experience of "primary disappointment" from which she may never recover when her innate expectation of what she will be a container and mother to is not realized. There is an absence of the phantasied beautiful baby, and, instead of a thinking link being formed and an ongoing effort being made to understand or know her baby (Bion's concept of "K", 1962a), reality is distorted, misrepresented, or denied. The baby is not seen for who it actually is and not only suffers from inadequate containment of its projections, but is often a receptacle for mother's projections of disappointment and loss.

Donald Meltzer, writing about "aesthetic reciprocity", suggests that a failure of emotional bonding between mother and infant results from some infants having been "overwhelmed by the aesthetic impact of the outside world and the prime object that represents it . . . the mother, her breasts and nipples, and her eyes and mind". Wondering why not all babies are so overwhelmed, he suggests that perhaps they all are, but some are saved, "in the nick of time", by something. What saves most normal babies from the overwhelming, crushing impact of their mother's beauty on them is the *reciprocal* power of the impact of the baby's beauty on the mother.

> In the same way as the mother's interior qualities of "motherliness" shine through her, delivering a "blow of awe and wonder to the baby", so the baby's interior qualities of "babyishness" deliver a corresponding blow to the parents. It is this capacity of the baby to ravish the mother with "love at first sight" that enables the baby to tolerate the aesthetic blow from the mother. If this does not happen and the baby cannot fill the mother with awe and love, it is unprotected from and overwhelmed by the aesthetic impact of its mother. [Meltzer, 1988: 45–58]

Meltzer goes on to describe a psychotherapy patient, Claudia, born physically and mentally handicapped, suggesting that the reason why Claudia was not saved, as most infants are, from being crushed by the aesthetic impact of her beautiful mother, was "because she experienced her mother seeing *her* as 'an ugly little clown'": in other words, because there was no reciprocal experience for the mother of being bowled over by the beauty of her baby.

Meltzer describes a session in Claudia's therapy, when she was 5, where she drew a clown, then whimpered: "It's ugly, throw it away!" The therapist talked about Claudia's feeling as a baby that "she was just an ugly, unhappy little clown", saying she would not throw the drawing away as it contained Claudia's valuable attempt to understand something. Claudia then cut out the clown, handing it and the remains of the cut-out cardboard to be kept in her folder. Meltzer felt that this was a crucial moment when "a new idea had been transmitted to the child that the beauty of an individual resides internally, in the qualities of the mind".

The birth of a damaged child had shocked Claudia's parents, and her mother, although dutiful,

> never gave the impression of seeing the spark of internal beauty in this child. Clearly something had been crushed, or in Claudia's imagery, she was a mother with a hole in her where a beautiful baby had been. For if the sheet of cardboard represents the body of the mother from which the ugly little clown

has been born, then what remains is a mother with a hole in her, as much in need of the therapist's help as the clown. [Meltzer, 1988: 45–58i]

Parents see their newborn as an aesthetic object. An experience of "primary disappointment" in the mother and the resulting failure of "aesthetic reciprocity" between mother and infant may underlie the profound difficulties of the following case.

Case history: "Sula"

Sula was referred when she was 6 by the social worker at the local school for severely mentally handicapped children. She was brain-damaged during a prolonged birth when she suffered oxygen deprivation. Sula had no speech, was walking but with poor motor control, and was epileptic. She was seen as very isolated and cut off, with autistic traits; she had screaming fits lasting for hours, yet she rejected physical comfort. The referral was precipitated by a crisis over a summer holiday, when Sula, who spent all day at a large play scheme, had become increasingly distressed and had begun self-mutilating and pulling her hair out.

There had been concerns about Sula since she was a baby, and the Social Services Department had been involved in supporting the family. Mother had suffered from depression after the birth and had been advised to spend time away from home, so she took a full-time job. Child-care arrangements were inadequate, and Sula was left with neighbours, and possibly alone at home, while her parents were out at work.

At the age of 4, Sula started attending the local school for severely mentally handicapped children, and initial worries there focused on her refusal to eat or drink hardly anything at school or at home. She was constipated and at times dangerously dehydrated and was close to hospital admission on several occasions.

In our meeting with the parents, the pain of having such a damaged child still seemed raw for mother, who wept while father remained silent and apparently detached. Mother recounted that her husband had been working abroad when Sula was born, returning to England when she was 6 months old. Mother had not realized she was pregnant until quite late and had been delighted at the news. At first the doctors had told her the baby was fine (although she had felt from the moment of birth that Sula was damaged), then had woken her to tell her that Sula was in the special care unit, where she remained for three months.

Mother expressed her breast-milk for ten weeks, but she claimed that the doctors had told her to stop because there was "something toxic" in the milk. A week later they changed their minds, but by then her milk had dried up. So at the point when Sula would have been able to breast-feed directly as opposed to being tube-fed her mother's milk, the breast was no longer available to her. Sula couldn't suck, and mother had to make holes in the teats of the bottles large enough to just pour the milk down her throat. At the time of referral the parents claimed that Sula could not chew or swallow food. She spat out all her food if they allowed her to sit up while she ate, so they held her lying down on the floor on her back and spooned liquidized food and water down her throat. It sounded like an intrusive, distressing procedure.

Sula had long epileptic fits, which were treated by the insertion of a suppository into her rectum. She was incontinent and in nappies. Night-times were exhausting, as Sula screamed for hours and hit her head, but her parents stressed that she could not cry tears. Their greatest pain was feeling that they could not comfort or cuddle her as she turned her back, tore up paper, or ripped at her skin. When I suggested she might be communicating anger, hurt, and frustration, they found this idea difficult to comprehend.

I agreed to see Sula for two individual assessment sessions; I describe the impact on me of my first encounter with her.

When I went to collect Sula from the waiting-room, I was struck by her thin body and unkempt hair framing her small round face. Her face was crisscrossed with scratches, scars, and raw patches where the skin had been ripped away. Her yellow teeth needed attention. Her back was crooked, and she was standing lopsided and panting heavily, moving her head around randomly, eyes unfocused. I was taken aback by the panting and asked father if they'd been running to get here. He said, "No, that's the way she breathes." I suggested she may be frightened coming here, but he said she was like that at home too. I thought to myself: "What a wreck." She swayed and clumped along, tapping with her hand along the wall of the corridor as if she were blind. She took my offered hand in her twisted hand, and I had to adjust to a strange grip. In the room she moved around and seemed to look not so much with her eyes, but by tapping ceaselessly at the furniture and the toys, panting, making strange utterances, and clumsily knocking things to the floor. Occasionally in her swaying her eyes would alight on me, but I didn't feel she was looking at me properly—a smile would appear, but it seemed to be from some sudden pleasure sensation, source unknown. Then she saw the paper laid out, excitedly took some and, panting and dribbling, began to tear it up. I said, "She's found something she knows, she does this at home too." I spoke to her about meeting her parents and how they had told me she gets upset sometimes. Talking to her felt silly, a waste of time, as she didn't seem to be "there" at all, with no sign of a mind that could take in what I was saying.

A lump of Plasticine fell, and she held the empty wrapping paper and began to feel it with her fingers. I started describing the crinkly feel and the sound the paper made as she explored it, but I soon stopped as I felt that something else was going on. She was fingering the paper delicately, working it up and down, folding it, rubbing it, panting more and more heavily, salivating, with little gasping sounds escaping her, and I felt that she was working herself up to a pitch of sexual excitement. She smiled, gave a loud shout, and seemed quite transported as she caressed the paper with increasing speed and intensity. At what seemed like a climax, she gave a loud shout of pleasure mixed with pain and terrible distress as she reached to her neck and hair, scratching and pulling at them and pinching her cheeks. I felt shocked by the intensity of her state of apparent sexual arousal and her distress and said, with some compassion in my voice, "It all feels too much for Sula, then she scratches herself. She gets so excited she doesn't know where she is, then she doesn't have to know about a new lady, new room, Daddy gone, she forgets it all." I was aware of my countertransference feeling that I would never remember the detail of the session, as if the shocking impact of my first contact with her could be swept away, just as Sula seemed to be masturbating away an unbearable feeling.

I began to feel that I couldn't bear seeing all the "proper" toys discarded on the floor as she fingered and licked the paper. I placed some unwrapped Plasticine near Sula, saying, "Sula might like to stop with the paper, stop being excited, but she's used to it, it fills her all up. What will she do if she stops?" For a moment her breathing quietened, she dropped the paper and explored a plastic cup, putting it to her lips. Intensely relieved, I wondered aloud if there was something she would be able to take in from her time here, like a good drink. Her eyes glanced at me for an instant, then, opening her legs out wide, she caressed and tickled herself, reaching under a corner of her nappy, panting, eyes closed.

Later she fell off a chair and flinched as I approached her, pushing me away and turning her back on me, to tap at the textures of the carpet and finger some discarded paper.

At one point she banged the scissors on the table, and it made a refreshing metallic sound. I took the scissors and tapped them on the table near her and then put my hand on the table, and she tapped near it; finally she gently patted my hand and our eyes met briefly. I said, "There is someone else here, interested in something different about Sula." I felt we had made some wholesome contact.

Soon I realized by the smell that Sula had defecated. She took out some Plasticine wodges, sniffed them excitedly, and, kneeling with her face at the level of the table, took a lump in her mouth, smiling and drooling. It was sickening, especially combined with the smell. She was excited by these great faecal masses of Plasticine, but all her zones and bodily orifices seemed to be confused, and I wondered whether this was linked to her refusal to eat and the intrusive insertion of suppositories into her anus during fits.

Discussion: processing the shock

I now felt I understood the panting that had so surprised me in the waiting-room, because it seemed to me that Sula was in a state of almost permanent sexual excitement. I thought it was possible that she had been or was currently being sexually abused, and it remained a question throughout my treatment of Sula. It was difficult to be sure about the meaning of Sula's eroticized behaviour, but I alerted the social worker, who shared my concerns. A case conference was convened, but no further action was taken as there was no clear evidence of abuse. The social worker continued to visit the home fairly regularly to meet with the parents and monitor the situation. As Sula's treatment progressed, the levels of sexual excitement diminished, and the school's and my concerns about current sexual abuse faded. I was uncomfortably aware that we were unlikely to gain a clearer picture of what may have happened to her in the past.

However, the point I wish to focus on was Sula's experience of unbearable sensations and feelings that seemed to overwhelm her. My sense of how intolerable it was to witness Sula's eroticization of everything in the room may have reflected a part of her that was experiencing something unbearable, perhaps an unconscious perception that she had given me a terrible shock when I met her. I had seen and allowed myself to think that this was a wreck, damaged beyond repair.

This first encounter and the feelings it engendered in me led me to imagine the first meeting between Sula and her mother. The shock and disappointment her mother still felt so keenly six years on must inevitably have been communicated to the baby, just as my response must at some level have communicated itself to Sula.

Autistic defences

I had not been able fully to process my feelings of shock when I met Sula, and perhaps this aggravated her state of distress. However, I think in the transference I was experienced as a potentially intrusive, uncontaining maternal object, resulting in Sula's retreat to an autistic type of sensual self-comforting, punctuated by brief moments of contact with me. Sula's tapping and use of her hands seemed to reflect this. At times the tapping seemed like a mindless ritual, an autistic feature, shutting out meaningful communication as well as unwanted intrusions. However, there were moments when I thought the tapping was more exploratory, containing possibly the germs of curiosity about her new situation and engendering some hope in me that a therapeutic relationship with her might be possible.

Paradoxically, when Sula was entering into her states of autoerotic arousal and losing contact with the outside world, her movements became smooth, delicate, and coordinated, in contrast to her clumsy lurchings around the room. Perhaps this was all she had to occupy her, and she was well practised in giving herself intensely pleasurable sensations. However, she quickly became overwhelmed with uncontainable feelings, and at the point of reaching a climax, her shouts were of pain more than pleasure, as if her feelings were bursting out of the holes she had picked in her skin. Her mutilated skin seemed to reflect a state of primitive "unintegration" (Bick, 1967), resulting from an extreme lack of early infantile containment, hampering the introjection of an internal skin container.

What seemed clear was that, besides the mental handicap and the possibility of sexual abuse, I was with a very disturbed, autistic type of child operating on an emotionally primitive level. Sula seemed to be living in a sensation-dominated world: the metal toy cars and hard table-top she ceaselessly tapped at and the soft paper she fingered were not so much objects as sources of hard and soft sensations. As Francis Tustin (1983) suggests: "These children carry hard objects around with them with which they feel equated. Thus by . . . turning their hard backs on people they engender sensations of being hard and impenetrable, sensations being of pre-eminent importance to such children" (p. 124). I think of Sula turning her back to her parents and her rigid rejection of any physical contact I offered her.

Tustin suggests that the attention of autistic children is so distracted from external reality by these "auto-generated sensations of hardness and softness that they appear to be deaf or even blind" (p. 125). This relates strongly to my impression that Sula behaved like a blind girl, concentrating on the sensations in her fingers, shutting out visual stimuli, and making herself impervious to contact.

Fluctuating states of mental handicap and the implications for treatment

As the assessment sessions progressed, I realized with a shock how difficult it was for me to keep my mind on Sula when she was not in a state of arousal but loping clumsily around the room, knocking things over and picking them up in an apparently random manner. It seemed as if she was so limited in her capacities that she could not really do much that could satisfy her or arouse my interest in her. What seemed to make it so difficult to attend to her was the lack of meaningful "patterning" and reciprocity of the kind established between a very young infant and her mother, since Sula's movements seemed to be lacking any form or meaning.

Yet I was struck by how, at moments, Sula seemed to be more accessible and also less handicapped. Jon Stokes (1987) has talked about patients moving in and out of handicapped states, linked to their fluctuating states of emotional integration and containment. This leads to questions about the nature of mental handicap and the type of treatment offered to disturbed handicapped children. If the primary handicap—the original damage—is overlaid by a secondary handicap, which may result from an extreme lack of containment of the baby's primitive communications by the mother, could a psychoanalytic approach to the treatment of severely handicapped children, where a model of maternal containment is offered, have a dramatic effect on the child's capacity to think and process her experiences? A striking feature of this case is how much change was effected in a relatively short period of time in once-weekly psychotherapy with a child as severely handicapped as Sula was. This could have implications for the type of child selected as suitable to benefit from the scarce resource of child psychotherapy.

Sula's therapy

I agreed to see Sula for once-weekly psychotherapy and to meet the parents once each term, as their working hours made it impossible for them to attend appointments regularly at the Clinic. I kept up close contact with the social worker and with the school, which played a central part in Sula's life, attending sensitively to her physical and emotional needs. I saw her on her own for 14 months before involving the rest of the family.

By the end of a year of treatment, reports from home and school were of a "changed child", no longer self-mutilating, who participated exuberantly in classroom activities, sought contact with adults and children, and accepted physical affection and comforting. She was eating school dinners, feeding herself, and was keen to be toilet-trained. I have attempted to assess what aspect of the therapy enabled Sula to make such dramatic improvements in a relatively short time, taking into account the damaged and distressed state she was in. I began to think in retrospect that what facilitated such change must be a certain kind of containment, the qualities of which I will try to explore, in conjunction with the thoughtful care she received at her specialist school.

The therapy can be divided into three phases. The first phase, like the assessment, was dominated by her autistic, cut-off states, intense eroticization, and fleeting moments of contact with me, which I tried to amplify while feeling hopeless about the extent of damage I was facing. The second phase was heralded by a sudden unavoidable break in the therapy and resulted in the threat of serious psychological breakdown. As Sula had gradually begun to shed her autistic defences and to make some emotional contact" with me, the sudden threat of the loss of her therapy seemed too much for her to bear. Her shrill cries of distress were replaced by the shedding of real tears, a communication of genuine sadness and upset, and, to her parents' delight, demands for cuddles and holding. Surviving the crisis, Sula went on to develop a capacity to elicit tender loving feelings towards her, both in me and in her teachers at school. I was able to get in touch with a beautiful baby Sula. This seemed to reflect Sula's capacity to introject a more loving internal object. This third phase heralded a move away from a primitive two-dimensional form of adhesive identification (sticking to the object in terror of being wrenched away or falling), which reached its height during her "breakdown" period, towards a more three-dimensional conception of an internal container. I will quote brief clinical extracts from Sula's therapy to illustrate these developmental phases within her psychoanalytic treatment.

First phase of therapy: filtering and amplifying

In her first therapy session Sula, breathing heavily as she looked around the room, gave the impression of being overwhelmed with stimulation. The therapy-room suddenly seemed too bright, too over-full of objects. She was like a little baby exposed to too many new sensations at once, and her writhing movements and rolling head seemed to be an attempt to shut out the intensity of the experience, as infants often do when intruded on by too many stimuli. What followed seemed like a dance between us composed of minute steps and movements, almost imperceptible at times, as I tried to help her filter the sensations she seemed to be overwhelmed by at one moment or completely shut off from at another. As she became more relaxed, Sula roamed around the room, shouting "Ah, ah, ah", which I took optimistically as I, I, I, and amplified for her, saying, "I, Sula, have come to get something for myself, my box, my chair." Sula stopped roaming, pulled her chair out, and sat herself in it. I began to feel hopeful about the tiny links she was making, although she did not look at me. I found myself being far more active than I am normally, and Sula responded, delighted when I rolled a toy car back to her, then amplified her shouts by making them into car noises. She sat forward, making a range of sounds, as if talking. However, there was always a piece of paper to hand for her to caress and fondle, and she reverted to this comfortable habit of auto-erotic stimulation, particularly when sudden unpredictable noises impinged in the room or when separation was imminent towards the end of the session.

In the light of Meltzer's ideas, I wonder whether in this session we can see a re-enactment of the impact of the aesthetic experience on the infant Sula from which she had not been rescued by a mother who could perceive her as beautiful. Sula clearly felt overwhelmed by the dazzling room at the beginning, like a tiny infant. Like Claudia's therapist, I too had to hold on to the potential for meaning and development in Sula as something valuable. I do not think I really believed Sula was speaking when she shouted "Ah", but felt it was important to attribute intentionality to her, where as yet there was none, and to lend meaning to her sounds, which may as yet have contained no meaning. It seemed important for Sula to have an experience of a maternal figure who could have faith in her and hope that she would one day be a talking little girl. Alvarez describes the importance for depressed or deprived children of phantasies of aspiration for future development. She talks about the act of reclaiming her autistic patient, Robbie, and the need to alert him to her alive, interested presence (Alvarez, 1992). I felt I had to reclaim Sula bit by bit in that session while struggling with my feelings of the futility of it all.

Projections of contamination

When Sula arrived at the door of the Clinic in her stained coat, with matted hair and scabbed face, pinching and shouting, I always felt a shock at seeing her and often wanted to give up working with her. I felt I was having to bear and contain Sula's outpourings of snot and dribble and with them evacuations of unprocessed sensations and feelings. The smell in the room was nauseating when she had defecated. She would mouthe and dribble over the toys, covering them with her saliva. I had powerful fantasies about Sula contaminating everything she touched.

I think I was meant to know about a baby Sula who felt she was perceived as disgusting and infectious—a monster baby that people could not wait to get rid of. In reality, her parents escaped as much as they could through their busy working lives. I dreaded the sessions with Sula and often hoped she would not come. Internally I was struggling with my feelings of disgust, having to acknowledge and confront them in myself. I also had to bear feelings of uselessness and impotence, feeling stupid and unskilled, and to try to understand these as countertransference communications from a severely damaged child.

The powerful effect on me of Sula's physical evacuations gave me some understanding of the difficulties her parents may have had in getting close to her physically and emotionally. This may have some bearing on Sula's difficulty in making meaningful connections and differentiating her needs clearly. One could imagine that the giving and receiving of clear messages between this mother and her baby had been severely hampered and that Sula's difficulties could be linked to her having internalized a confused and confusing maternal object.

At this stage I felt that Sula had no real idea of a space inside her or inside anyone else that could contain her feelings; instead, they were evacuated out, in an unprocessed form, and just happened to be picked up by me. Sula also seemed to take things into herself indiscriminately. I think this may link not only to her possible sexual abuse and the idea that she may have had nasty and exciting things put into her in all the wrong orifices, compounded by her treatment for fits (the suppository in her anus), but to her earliest feeding relationship with her mother, who was led to believe she was feeding something toxic to her baby.

From the beginning there had been confusion in mother and in Sula about what is good or bad to take in. Now Sula rejected the toys in favour of scrap rubbish or chewing bits of Plasticine. She rejected cuddles and warmth from her parents as if they were dangerous and spat out proper food as if it were poison. She opted for auto-erotic excitement in place of a nourishing emotional contact with me. Although these words—"opt", "reject", "choose"—suggest conscious decisions, I do not think this was the case initially; it is difficult to find the language to describe the undifferentiated confusion of Sula's world.

Emerging intelligence

Over time I detected a growing awareness of her actions in Sula, and on occasion she became deliberately provocative, choosing familiar but perverse means of gratification in preference to wholesome but uncertain contact with me. For example, she sometimes pushed her pencil up her nose, deliberately holding the snot-filled end near her mouth as she looked at me. This felt like a deliberate communication of her need to test out my capacity to contain all aspects of Sula, including the most unsavoury ones, as well as to establish my capacity to be firm and set limits to her behaviour.

As time went on, Sula's awareness of me in the room increased: instead of using my chair to tap and touch, she would come up to me and put her hand suggestively on my thigh, stroking it. I felt that she was looking for a way of making contact with me and was becoming more interested in relatedness, although she still focused mainly on sensory experiences. I found it helped if I was firm, and I noticed that her intelligence seemed to increase.

> In one session five months into her therapy, she bit off a piece of her rubber and began chewing it. My usual comments about the wrong stuff going into her mouth were not heard, and I began to worry that she could swallow it and choke. I opened her mouth, got it out, and, undeterred, she placed it in her mouth again! This battle for control continued for some time, and I persisted in stopping her from chewing it. Suddenly she stopped putting it into her mouth, sat up, and stared at me silently, with an enigmatic smile. She looked beyond me at the window and around the room, head held high. For a moment she looked quite different, more beautiful, and had a real intelligence in her eyes. I was so struck by this, I said: "Sula's looking around her with new eyes, maybe there's a way of using her mouth for other things, to talk even." She sat leaning towards me, mouth open as if she wanted to tell me something, and I leant forward, attentive and listening.

I thought that she experienced my stopping her as containing, and this extended to my physical holding of her hands later to prevent her from hurting herself. Her intelligent look, revealing the beauty of a developing mind, could be linked to her feeling that someone was paying close enough attention and cared enough to stop her being destructive and treating herself as if she were rubbish.

Second phase of therapy: breakdown or breakthrough?
Awareness of psychic pain

A shift in Sula's development seemed to occur quite suddenly when, arriving at the Clinic after a missed session, father told me that a relative had died in their home country, and they were returning the following day for several weeks. He also reported with delight that Sula was sitting on her mother's lap, asking for cuddles. I quote briefly from the session that followed:

> Sula stood in the doorway dripping snot and putting one then two fingers up her nose. Her coat was caked with dirt, and she looked very upset. I said, "Sula's come feeling in a real mess", and wiped her nose. She tapped at the dolls' house and some dolls fell to the ground. I spoke about the dolls that fell down, gone—maybe she thought I was gone last week when she didn't come. Now she is going away, and she will come back. She tapped at the doll people. I held up a doll baby and doll mother, put the baby in the mother's arms, and said, "Sula's liking cuddles from her Mummy now." She began breathing heavily but soon became very distressed. She stood, eyes shut tight, and wept in a heartbroken way. It was the first time I had seen her cry tears of abject misery and unhappiness, unlike the shouts of before. I remembered that her parents had told me how Sula had never cried tears before. I talked about how she was feeling upset and sad today, but her crying became frightened, and I talked of her fear—fear of dropping like the dolls, falling. . . . Eventually she calmed down, opened her eyes, and I took her on my lap; soon her fingers strayed to my thigh, and she stroked it. I stopped her, put her on her own chair, and she played quietly for a while.

Although extremely painful to witness, it seemed to me as if Sula was in some way becoming more alive and human, as circumstances and our work together imposed some kind of challenge to her system of autistic evasions and auto-eroticism, forcing her to be more in touch with feelings of utter grief about parting, separation, loss, and damage. In retrospect it felt as if this was the most dangerous period for Sula as she emerged from a cut-off state, where she had dealt with unpleasant experiences by evacuating them, often bodily. Now she was having to face a psychic knowledge of unbearable truths that might prove too much for her. Could the breakdown lead to a breakthrough, or, deprived of her defences, would Sula resort to the kind of fragmentation of reality into such tiny bits that the prospect of recovery is very slight (Bion, 1967a)?

It seemed as if at moments Sula could begin to conceive of a space that was not filled up with toxic stuff and a mother's lap that might even be welcoming to her, but with this came the painful recognition of losses past and present, awareness of what she had never had, and the absence of the holding lap/mind during separation. It was clear, however, that the notion of an internal containing space was only just beginning as an idea, and that under emotional pressure Sula resorted to operating at a more primitive level. Her sensual stroking of my thigh quickly replaced another kind of holding, by my lap, eyes, and mind.

Breakdown

Sula moved from momentary states of feeling contained by me to a more two-dimensional adhesive form of identification (Meltzer, 1975b), sticking to the surface of objects, clinging on as if her survival depended on it. This latter mode became more extreme on her return from their trip, five weeks later, as recognition of her separateness and fundamental aloneness filled her with a primitive terror of fragmentation and falling into nothing:

> Father reported that he thought Sula felt insecure, as now she wanted to hold his hand constantly. Sula refused to release his hand until she had a firm grip on mine. She could hardly bear the brief transition to the room and stood inside, screaming and crying as if she was falling apart. The entire side of her face was raw and mutilated, and her hands were stained with blood from scratching. I spoke soothingly to her, holding both hands tight in mine and telling her I was not going to let her hurt herself. She calmed down and went into a dreamlike trance, staring ahead—into the dolls' house. I tried to move her to her

seat, but as I loosened my grip on one hand, she would reach to her face and tear at it, crying in panic and fear. She seemed to feel as if she was falling apart unless she was being physically held.

After a long time I got up and, holding on to her all the time, pushed a chair under her. As she seemed to cope with that, I took a ball out of the box with one hand. I put the ball into her hands, moving them into position, as if she were a baby learning how to take a rattle. She passed the ball back and forth to me, as if rehearsing tiny separations and transitions in space, growing increasingly confident.

I think it is clear from this material how catastrophic the disruption to her routine was felt to be. Sula used the second-skin defences (Bick, 1967) that tiny babies resort to when they feel in danger of falling to pieces and lack internal or external containment. Sula entered a trance-like state, fixing her eyes to one spot in the room, in an attempt to hold herself together. The ripping of her skin can be understood as a communication of how she felt violently torn away from those she needed to be close to, literally as if her skin were being stripped from her.

It was distressing to see Sula so upset, and it brought to mind a head-banging patient of Sinason's who, as he lost his secondary handicaps and thus his defences against meaning, began to cry pitifully in his sessions. She says:

> It is a weeping to do with a terrible sense of aloneness and the reality of that. Neville Symington has commented that weeping comes when there is a breakthrough with this kind of patient and represents a real awareness of all the meaning that has been lost in the years up to that moment as well as the aloneness of handicap. [Sinason, 1992a]

Sinason was concerned that therapy might be too cruel for her patient and quotes Shirley Hoxter's comments on the ethical issues involved in the treatment of physically ill and disabled children: "The pains of integration may be worthwhile when they lead to 'ordinary human unhappiness, but we feel guilty and cruel if integration seems only to offer the sufferance of suffering" (Hoxter, quoted by Sinason, 1992a). Sinason's patient worked through this state, and the crying stopped. Similarly, Sula responded to the containment offered to her and survived this period in her therapy. The experience proved to be a spur to her development and seemed to confirm the value of psychoanalytic therapy for a child as damaged as Sula. She remained cognitively limited and very disabled, but many of her secondary handicaps fell away, along with the intense levels of distress that had been assumed to be a part of or caused by her primary handicap.

Third phase of therapy: breakthrough

In this phase of her therapy, Sula demonstrated an increasing ability to bear separations without needing to render herself mindless: for example, following her father's exit from the Clinic with her eyes, then turning away and coming calmly to the room with me. She seemed to want to be helped to stop scratching her skin, which she resorted to increasingly out of habit. She began to spit copiously in the room, shooting out great arcs of saliva and wetting everything within reach. This activity began to annoy me intensely, as it was clear that she was doing it deliberately. She would go off calmly at the end of a session, leaving me with her mess. The capacity to split and project her aggressive feelings into me represented a development for Sula, who now had some respite from her negative feelings, as she expelled whatever she felt was toxic within her in order to take in the nourishment being offered to her in her external life. However, this splitting was not totally successful, as suddenly in the middle of some activity, for no apparent external reason, Sula would be seized with a fit of inconsolable distress.

I think this spurting of saliva may have had sexual connotations as well. Although Sula's eroticization had diminished considerably, it was still an open question whether Sula had been sexually abused. It was clear that she had been exposed to adult sexuality, having slept for most of her life in a cot in her parents' or grandparents' bedroom. In any event I began to think that Sula's masturbatory activities, her intrusive sticking of her fingers into her nose and nappy and her occasional biting of my hand, might be an unconscious attack on her object through projective identification, "spoiling its beauty, resulting in identification with an ugly object"

(Meltzer, 1988). This perverse sexuality could be seen as an identification with an ugly, hateful intercourse, which, in phantasy, could produce a hateful baby (despite the fact that the damage was not congenital). Sula, unable to talk, can perhaps only express implicitly the kinds of questions Meltzer formulates in relation to the aesthetic impact of the mother and baby on each other and what happens when the love at first sight is not, for whatever reason, mutual:

> "What kind of conjunction of my parents has produced this either ugliness or feeling of ugliness?" The response might be: "... if my parents cannot convey to me that they experience me as beautiful, I cannot then imagine myself to be the product of a beautiful and mysterious conjunction, but only of an ugly secret one". [Meltzer, 1988]

One might consider whether the parental intercourse could be perceived, in phantasy, to be one of harmful intent. Was Sula's turning away from the apparently toxic breast-milk linked to a phantasy of a parent couple who may have had ambivalent feelings towards keeping her alive, and could this have contributed to her ongoing feeding difficulties?

I think there may have been a similar ambivalence about acknowledging that Sula was growing up. I have noticed, in other cases, a tendency for parents to over-protect their damaged children, wrapping them in layers of clothing, for example, perhaps in compensation for their hostile wishes but also because, as they grow older, the gap widens between their developmental capacities and those of normal children. Mother told me that, although she had an 18-month-old son, "Sula is the real baby". Although they felt Sula could not chew and needed baby food, it was more likely that she was choosing not to chew and colluding with their wish to keep her as the baby in the family, and the same applies to her apparent incontinence.

The beautiful baby

In her sessions it was becoming clear that Sula had begun to internalize a containing, thinking, and lively object. She began to enjoy herself in the room, playing like a toddler. On one occasion she stood and banged on her toys, looked at me, and smiled in a lively way. She tried to sit, and I got up to help her, noticing that she smelt fresh and clean, although her face was still marked. I said: "Sula is smelling nice and clean today, she seems to be feeling good inside too. She can be a girl it feels nice to be near." She took the baby doll down from the shelf and made as if to shove it into her mouth. I tensed, thinking it would be covered with her saliva. But she sat at the foot of my chair, kneading it gently and looking up at me, smiling. Feeling tender towards her, I leaned down closer to her and said: "Sula feels she can be my lovely therapy baby here today." She sat calmly for the last few minutes of the session.

After a year of treatment, the school reported many significant changes, including those I mentioned earlier. Sula insisted on being fed her school dinners and then began to eat with her fingers and drink small amounts. She enthusiastically initiated communication with adults and children, using her eyes, hands, and voice expressively. She was happily integrated into her class, had begun to smile, and the general feeling was of a child with a mind, however damaged, beginning to emerge. Her teacher described Sula running up to her and offering her face for a kiss. Sula would glance up at the teacher to see her reaction—did she feel she was kissing a monster or a loveable child? The teacher told me she felt loving towards Sula and kissed her sincerely. I think Sula was moving towards seeing herself as part of the "class of beautiful babies" (Meltzer, 1988).

In trying to consider what it was that may have contributed to alleviating Sula's distress, I suggest that, against a background of close liaison between school, social worker, and Clinic, which provided some containment for the parents' distress, Sula was able to make use of the containment offered in the therapy. I think that by allowing myself to experience and acknowledge feelings of disgust and horror at this child, who felt herself to be an infectious monster, I was providing a container for her most unbearable projections to find a home—a mind to begin thinking about them. As I struggled with my feelings, which were murderous too, in the sense of wishing to get rid of her, I could allow myself to notice the initially minute signs of a more beautiful "interior" in Sula's moments of curiosity and try to amplify these. In this sense I am not sure that, as the title suggests, we were facing the damage together.

I think I was meant to experience and face the impact of the damage on her behalf, to contain and think about it. The point of near-breakdown came when Sula began to feel that there was an object worth clinging onto for her survival and from whom she could not bear to be wrenched away. Having survived the terror of disintegration, Sula became increasingly able to look to others for help and to care for herself. It did not seem to be coincidence that Sula was demanding to be toilet-trained at this time.

Family work

In discussion with the school, social worker, and parents, we agreed that I would end Sula's individual therapy with a term's notice. I would continue to see Sula in the context of her family, together with the social worker, to try and enable them to think about Sula's difficulties within the family and to give them a space to think about their own mental pain. Mother did not attend, as she was still working long hours, but father attended with Sula and her siblings. The transformation in father was particularly remarkable. He was very distant and detached to begin with, but over time, and by watching the detailed way in which we commented on Sula's communications, he began to share some of his observations with us about the dreadful sleepless nights they continued to have. Sula was sent off to bed long before the other children, because she screamed for hours before going to sleep. The logic was that if they did not let her start screaming early enough, she would get to sleep even later. Father described how Sula would cry sadly and hit her head with her fist: "When she hits her head, it's like she's hitting my heart", he said, touching his chest poignantly. As father described staying up with Sula all night, since she could not bear to be alone, Sula was feeling an empty box, and she began to tear at her hair. The empty box seemed to evoke a bereft, desolate feeling in her, and I wondered about her awareness of something missing in her, a good internal object to hold onto, especially at night. She was finding it difficult to face the emptiness and damage on her own. As we were discussing this problem, Sula gave us a demonstration of the night-time experience. Lying in a half-awake, half-asleep state on the floor, she began crying, pulling at her hair with one hand and hitting her head with the other. "That's it, that's exactly what she does!" shouted father, relieved to be able to share it with us.

A few weeks later father reported a dramatic change, saying that Sula was insisting on staying up with her siblings in the evening, was going to bed peacefully at 9.00 p.m., and sleeping through the night. It appeared that on some level Sula had been able to take in her father's increased mental availability to her. This enabled her to relinquish his concrete presence with her throughout the night.

In conclusion, I have tried to show through my work with Sula how the experience of "primary disappointment" in a mother, when her expectation of a healthy baby is not realized, can have a profound effect on the attachment process between mother and baby. The mourning process in that situation is seldom completed, and the infant not only suffers from inadequate containment of her projections, but is often the receptacle for mother's projections of disappointment and loss. This is an important factor in the formation of a "secondary handicap" (Sinason, 1992a, 1992c). The work with Sula illustrates the ideas expressed about the importance of maternal containment in early infancy, and Meltzer's thoughts about the aesthetic impact of mother and baby on each other.

CHAPTER FIVE

Learning disability as a refuge from knowledge

David Simpson

My work with people who have learning disabilities has led me to the conclusion that a major factor adding to their difficulties and preventing their learning and development is the way in which their disability can act as a refuge from knowledge.

The current use of the term "learning disability" in the United Kingdom, replacing "mental handicap" or "mental retardation" to refer to those people with limited intelligence (IQ score below 70), has added to this problem by increasing confusion. This term obscures the distinction between constitutional low intelligence in which organic disorder and inheritance are significant determinants and difficulties in learning of a psychological origin. This distinction is important because these two entities so frequently overlap, and they can also masquerade as each other. The overlap is seen in mentally retarded people who show psychological diffi-

---

This chapter has previously appeared in the *Journal of Psychoanalytic Psychotherapy*, 16 (2002, no. 3): 215–226. The Journal's website can be found at <www.tandf.co.uk>.

culties in using the intelligence they have; sometimes this is called "secondary handicap" (Sinason 1992b).

The masquerade occurs in two directions:

First, among people considered to have learning disabilities, there is a significant group whose innate intelligence is within the normal range or even above average. They may have depressed IQ scores or behave as if they are learning disabled, but they actually have a normal IQ on testing. This is what I mean by "masquerading": in these cases, difficulties in learning of psychological origin are masquerading as mental retardation. In my experience many of these people have undiagnosed psychiatric illnesses—particularly borderline personality disorder, but also neuroses and psychoses. The prevalence of schizophrenia in those with mild mental retardation is three times that in the general population.

Second, in the opposite direction, mental retardation can masquerade as psychological difficulties in learning. The gross examples are rare and usually occur in situations where a parent does not accept the child's organic defects and, instead, clings to what they believe is a more hopeful diagnosis of psychological learning difficulties. These cases may have an extreme quality, when a child is believed to have hidden special abilities and the parents are often militant. Sometimes the diagnosis of autism is used in this way. At a more subtle level, the problem is more ubiquitous.

The very use of the term "learning disability" paves the way to this masquerade, and the danger for those taking a psychological view on mental retardation is that we are prone to this trap. Unless we are clear in our minds about what we are dealing with, we run the risk of obscuring the organic problems of our patients. Conversely, when psychological difficulties in learning are masquerading as mental retardation, the problem is very similar. Again, the term "learning disability" can obscure a clear distinction between the two, and in this case I suspect that what is evaded are the implications of making a psychiatric diagnosis.

In both these situations, I consider that the term "learning disability" has been used as a refuge from knowledge. I believe that behind this is a fear of learning the truth. To know the reality of organic deficit or of psychological/psychiatric difficulties, both with implications of irreparable damage, would be too traumatic for all concerned: for the patient and their relatives, as well as for ourselves. As professionals, we are in danger of enacting this situation where there is a powerful need to protect somebody from knowing the truth. This is a problem that lies at the psychological core of many people with learning disabilities. The origin of this problem is the focus of this chapter, and I examine this from a psychoanalytic perspective.

From a clinical point of view, this problem highlights the importance of making a thorough diagnostic assessment, including a psychological assessment and, where feasible, a psychiatric evaluation, for people with learning disabilities, if psychoanalytic psychotherapy is considered. The problem with being diagnosticians is that we are often purveyors of bad news, and as such we share something with the mentally handicapped who, I suspect, often believe that their very existence is bad news. In situations when knowledge means knowing deficit—that is, what we do not have or cannot do, rather than what we do have or can do—learning presents a profound problem.

Psychoanalysis is useful in providing theories for understanding the origin of learning; I use these to illuminate the nature of some of the difficulties in learning seen in people with learning disabilities and include my ideas about the way that their learning disability may fit with a defensive organization that acts as a refuge from knowledge. I illustrate these points in my discussion of clinical material from my work with an adolescent boy.

Psychoanalytic perspectives

In Freud's (1911b) view, the development of the ego, including the capacity to learn, depends on there being a shift in mental life from the dominance of the pleasure principle to the dominance of reality principle. In his view, thought develops as a response to the need to bridge the gap between the experience of a desire and its satisfaction, which is necessary for this transition to take place. The transition from the pleasure principle, where there is a desire for immediate gratification, to an adjustment to reality, where there is an acceptance of the necessary struggle to meet our conflicting needs, is not at all easy. It begins in infancy and continues throughout life. In Bion's (1962b) view, the capacity to make this transition and to learn from experience depends upon our capacity to tolerate frustration.

Those of us who are learning disabled find this transition very difficult. I believe that there are two very important reasons for this, over and above organic deficit. First, the capacity of people with learning disabilities to tolerate frustration, in which constitutional factors play an important part, is often restricted. Second, and not least, the reality that people with learning disabilities have to face is very difficult to bear. This reality includes not only the external objective facts of their life, including their disability, but also their internal reality: the thoughts, feelings, and imaginings inside their minds and—of particular importance—their social reality; their internal worlds, and the specific responses of other people, particularly their parents.

Klein (1928), like Freud (1909d, 1916–17), considered the epistemophilic instinct or desire for knowledge, which includes curiosity, to be a component of infantile sexual instinct. She believed that the instinct for knowledge followed the child's sadistic desires to enter, possess, and destroy its mother's body, activated by its awakening Oedipus complex. The desire to know is secondarily reinforced by the need of the child to master the considerable anxiety engendered. Anxiety can, however, inhibit the desire to know if the damage to the mother is believed to be too great.

This conveys a very vivid picture. However, I also consider that the way in which the mother/parent responds to the child's curiosity in terms of their overall and often subtle emotional attitude is of greater importance than Klein stressed.

Children are particularly sensitive to the way their parents may show pleasure and interest in their curiosity or may be embarrassed, hurt, guilty, or merely unresponsive. In addition, a central concern of children is the nature of their parents' relationship, and their parents' attitude to each other and the child's effect on this, including through the act of being curious. Knowing this reality is one of the original objects of the child's curiosity, and that, as a result of this, powerful forces arise that can either impede the growth of knowledge or allow it to flourish.

Oedipal conflict is central, both between the child and his parents and also through the child's experience of the oedipal situation inside his parents' minds. The extent to which a parent can tolerate curiosity in the child if their curiosity is coloured with destructive or sadistic phantasies depends upon the individual parent's capacity to tolerate her/his own phantasies in this respect, which is a function of the extent to which they have been able to work through their own oedipal conflict.

This perspective helps to shed light on the psychological difficulties in learning faced by many people with learning disabilities over and above their considerable limitations. A disability—particularly a learning disability—is very difficult for any parent to bear in their child, and it mobilizes very powerful psychological defences. When faced with a handicapped child, most parents experience intense pain, which includes a powerful sense of shame and persecutory guilt. Their guilt usually relates, in my view, to a belief that at some level they are responsible for their child's handicap.

The most common defence is denial. This is not a blatant denial of reality, although this is sometimes the case, but, rather, a more subtle disavowal of the nature and extent of the problem. A gross example of this might be seen in cases where mental handicap becomes masqueraded as special ability. However, the more subtle situation is much more commonplace and often unnoticed, although sometimes betrayed in phrases such as "She's a rewarding challenge", "He's always with me", and even "He's such a loving child".

In many case these defences hold off and perpetuate an underlying state of chronic depression in the parents. This is a melancholic state in which the mourning of losses that result from having a handicapped child, and which may include the loss of the child who was hoped for and imagined, is arrested because of the enormity of the pain and guilt that it threatens. This melancholic state often hangs like a black cloud over the relationship between the parents, which so often deteriorates through the weight of guilt and shame: at some level, their very sexual acts may be held responsible for all their family's problems.

The most important problem faced by a child in this situation is not overt hostility from the parents, although this does occur, but of having parents who cannot bear to know reality, particularly their child's reality. The child then fears that, if it shows curiosity towards its parents, instead of gaining self-affirming interest, it will engender considerable discomfort by way of shame and guilt, hostility, or even catastrophe. The child becomes a burden to its parents, and its parents become a burden to the child. This situation puts pressure on the child to fit in with the parents' defences so that its learning disability becomes a refuge from reality. The child then disavows its desire for knowledge. This is vividly seen in those who cannot look at you for fear of meeting your gaze.

As O'Shaughnessy (1981) describes Bion's view, the first form of thinking is a struggle to know psychic qualities and is the outcome of the early emotional events between a baby and its mother. Thinking is not an abstract mental process but an emotional experience dependent upon a human link with the aim of understanding oneself and others. In this view, we can only know ourselves through experience of being known by others. For the person with learning disability, this is very difficult and they actively turn away from reality, anticipating an object that cannot bear to know them.

Clinical material: "Sam"

I treated this patient in weekly individual psychotherapy for two-and-a-half years.

Background

Sam was 15 years old when referred. He has a severe learning disability. His family were from abroad and had moved to Britain soon after his birth. As a result of his special needs, including his parents' difficulties in managing him, he had lived in a residential school since he was young. He remained in contact with his parents and brother through regular daytime visits at weekends.

At the time of the referral, his behaviour had become very challenging. He was absconding and had become increasingly agitated and obsessional. He normally desired routine but was now compulsively touching and licking, anally masturbating, and smearing faeces. His sleep was disturbed, and he would wander about the home at night. He had lost weight; and his speech, normally limited to simple repetitive phrases, had deteriorated. In class he could no longer work. His teachers reported that excited, overactive periods were not infrequent and lasted for days to weeks, with recovery in-between.

Sam's appearance and behaviour, which make him stand out, suggest that he is mentally handicapped. He has slanted eyes, simply formed large ears, and teeth that slant backwards. When these features are considered together with his limited speech, which is cluttered and perseverative, and his obsessional socially aversive behaviour, the suggestion is that he was born with "fragile X syndrome". This results from a chromosomal abnormality that is the commonest heritable cause of mental retardation. Although Sam had had a blood test for this syndrome in the past and this had proved negative, modern tests are more accurate; but a repeat test was prevented by Sam's aversion to needles. Although there was no certain diagnosis, it was clear to me—and, I strongly suspect, to his family and carers—that Sam has a profound inborn organic impairment in his intellectual ability and his potential for further development.

Assessment

I met a tall, red-haired boy with a blank smile that quickly faded. Remarkably, he offered me his hand to shake, and I held his long trembling fingers. He moved about the room in a jumpy way, picking things up and making a sharp staccato utterance, "Duk, Duk, Duk". He shuffled papers and made a mark with a pen, but no more.

Out of the toy box, he picked a child doll and dropped it; and then a woman doll, and started unwinding the dress, quickly dropped this, becoming agitated, and with a cry left the room, intruding into other rooms on his way back to the care-worker. I was struck by vivid glimpses of meaningful contact interspersed in his agitated searching.

At the second visit, he was even more agitated, but when he said, "James", his teacher's name, he showed relief when I said that I thought he was upset because James was away.

At this time his agitation and sleeplessness was increasing, and the local consultant child psychiatrist prescribed a tranquillizer. During two further interviews, Sam was much less agitated and more able to stay with me and to speak.

The local psychiatrist believed that Sam had recurrent manic episodes and prescribed a mood-stabilizing drug. From a psychodynamic point of view, at the time of his assessment, I considered that he used manic and related obsessional defences to control anxiety. He was particularly vulnerable to loss and became agitated when his teacher was away and when there were breaks in treatment. However, what were the sources of Sam's anxiety?

I was uncertain about recommending psychotherapy for Sam, and what led me to decide in favour of it, over and above the points of good contact that I had with him during the assessment, was the overall support in the network and particularly that the local psychiatrist was involved. Initially, I offered a six-month trial.

The course of treatment

He came to see me eagerly, and in the early parts of the sessions he appeared much less anxious. In the beginning he concentrated on the toy box; and, in what became a routine, he pulled out a set of dolls that corresponded with his own family. There was a baby doll, "Baby Sam", which he held tightly and stroked on his lips. There was a mother doll that he often held with its feet on the baby doll's head. Less frequently, a father doll appeared, and a little boy, whom he called by his brother's name. I got a glimpse of something that did not really develop, and I was left expectant.

The fact that this became a routine and that I tended to concentrate on it created a safe area for Sam away from sources of anxiety, which are always around. This emerged towards the end of sessions and/or if the more routine play did not develop; and if I tended to be more active in enquiry towards Sam, then he became jumpy, would get up, and go to the door to leave. This "going to the door" was a major feature of the routine: some sessions were dominated by it, and I was occupied in trying to understand it. Usually he would return to his seat if I asked him to stay. If more anxious, he would stand at the door, sometimes leaving it open. If he went out, he usually returned repeatedly with the phrase "see you Thursday", the day of the session.

He was very frightened of being trapped: but by what? There were moments of intense fear. He would point to the window and appear frightened of something he could see in the shadow of the trees or the reflection. It felt as if there was a frightening external presence. With time this became much more clearly located in me and most intense when we broke through a barrier of familiarity. I think he was very frightened of me. Although he could get some relief when I spoke simply to show that I had understood him, this was short-lived, and as his anxiety rose, he would tend to turn away and be silent or to bolt for the door. At times he found it easier when I was more silent but not totally silent, because this was also frightening.

He found contact with me almost unbearable, even when I understood him. I believe he was frightened of being known by me: that I would learn more about him than he was accustomed to showing. He was particularly anxious not to impinge on me with his curiosity, although he monitored me closely and was acutely sensitive to changes in me. There were some surprising moments of enlightenment. Early in treatment I made a mistake with his name when he was going to the door, and he swung round and said "Sam" with surprising alertness.

He kept me at a safe distance and under tight control. He placated me, threatening to reject me by leaving but usually looking for my approval and permission. When he was brought by James, he became anxious to leave me and could play me off against James. There was also the quandary that he put me in. Do I let him go? Or shut the door? He was an adolescent: he could see the quandary and would tease me and laugh about it. He would also be angry and assertive about it. I think he had noticed that opening the door had the effect of inhibiting me from speaking, with a corridor of people passing, so he found a way to censor my words!

Signs of adolescence were very important. Although they were signs of progress, they were disturbing and presented Sam and other people with problems as they were in the realm of what Sam was frightened would be known.

During his treatment with me, symptomatically Sam improved. His agitation decreased, his speech developed, and he became more like a teenager.

*Extract of a session with Sam
(after one year of psychotherapy)*

Sam was sitting away from his escort in a full waiting-room. He looked at me and said in a high-pitched voice, "Dddd... it's Dr Simpson." Everybody looked at me. I nodded to him, and there was a delay before he got up; then I said "Hello" as we moved out the door. He repeated "Dr Simpson... dddd... Hello, Dr Simpson, it's Thursday, it's Thursday, see you Thursday." He lagged behind as we went down to my room, repeating these phrases and adding "James". He picked up the toy box, which he then rummaged through until he picked out a baby and a mother doll and began stroking the baby doll's head with the mother doll's feet, sometimes stroking his lip with the baby doll.

He smiled at me and then quickly looked out of the window. He then surreptitiously took a male figure out of the toy box and said, "Hello, Dr Simpson, it's Thursday." I said, "You are keeping me safe, playing as you always do with the dolls like this, which is safe." He said "Yes", staring at me, putting his hand onto the heating pipe behind. I said, "You are keeping your distance because you are not sure whether I am hot or cold." He smiled and then stared out of the window.

He began fingering the dolls, putting the baby doll underneath his jumper. When I showed interest in this, he looked away. I said, "The dolls are safe, much safer than finding out about me and what else is here." He looked down, and I said, "I think you are interested here but are frightened to show it." He said, "Sam" (which reminded me of the previous session where I had mistaken his name). I said, "You are frightened that if you become interested in what is around you here you will lose my interest and you will have to remind me that it is you, Sam, not somebody else that I am seeing." After a pause, "But also you are frightened of really looking at me." He began staring into space. I said, "You are stuck between me and trying to move away, which are both frightening." He then seemed quieter and held a male figure, which I recognized as the father. He muttered "Primrose Lane" (his school) and smiled. Then I felt he wasn't able to look at me directly and said, "Now you can't look into my eyes for fear of what you might see" and, after a slight pause, "and you are frightened of what I might say, which makes it difficult to speak". There was a silence of several minutes, while he fumbled with the toys. I said, "It is very difficult just to be here with me" and he said, "Yeah", looking at me. To my surprise, my telephone rang, and I answered it briefly. Afterwards he seemed more jumpy, and I said, "You've been upset by the telephone." He nodded and said, "James". I asked him whether James was still at work. He nodded, and I said, "You are worried about James being ill." He said, "Ill, yes ... no, no." I said, "James is important now because you are worried about him; but I you are also worried about me, especially when things can take me away."

He brought out a blue beaker and repeated, "Blu ... blu ..."; then he picked up the father doll and sat looking out of the window and seemed sad. He then picked up the mother doll and the baby doll, putting the father doll down; I said, "You are showing me your sadness at no longer being a child who plays with toys and no longer living with your family." I was about to say that I reminded him of what he missed, but he quickly said, "Sunday". I said, "Yes, you see them on Sunday, but you don't live with them, and you feel sad about that and you are just beginning to feel that I could look at this." However, he had moved away and brightly repeated, "It's Thursday, bye ... it's Thursday, bye Dr Simpson." He left and sat in the hallway with his escort coming to get him.

Discussion

During this session, up until the telephone interruption, Sam is very inhibited. He is preoccupied with my state, and this preoccupation is in the maternal transference. Sam's difficulty in showing curiosity is central. He believes that being curious is very dangerous, and he tries to rid himself of it, becoming inhibited when I am curious about him. I suspect he believes his curiosity to be dangerous because of his fear of what it might evoke in me, as he feared what it might evoke in his mother, in particular that it might have engendered shame, guilt, or admonishment.

He is frightened both for and of his object, which I suspect he views as vulnerable. He seeks a close relationship with me, literally skin-to-skin, and that when we are in a familiar routine, he can find this with me. In this state his curiosity is disavowed and hidden, and he becomes the handicapped little child who never grows up. He is, however, extremely cautious of me and is terrified of what he might see and what my reaction might be if he and I were to come alive.

Although Sam is inhibited by my curiosity about him, he is at the same time particularly sensitive to anything that might disrupt my attention to him, which further increases his inhibition. He becomes very anxious following my answering the telephone. However, he is relieved when I interpret his fear of losing contact, which leads to a freer sequence of material in which he is able to show me, momentarily, his sadness.

From the transference, I have the impression of a mother who watches him but can bear to see only an infant. He is terrified of disturbing her and feels that he must fit in with her image of him as a handicapped infant. In this situation it feels to me as if infancy and childhood are being held on to like a saving grace or blessing, with even a promise of immortality, the price of which is the handicap itself. I suspect that, in phantasy, imperfection is then magically converted to perfection. The cost, however, of time standing still is that development cannot occur. The mother's disillusionment, when faced with her real child, and her grief and mourning for what was hoped for in the face of its disability, are obliterated. For Sam, not fitting in with her defensive system may have a heavy price, including being ignored completely.

I am not saying that his mother is not aware of the facts of his being handicapped; but I suspect she disavows these at an emotional level, seeing him simultaneously as handicapped and not handicapped. The implication of this is that the problem is not primarily a question of information about Sam's condition, but of the difficulty of accepting this.

Sam rarely uses the word "Mummy", which fits with a skin-to-skin closeness where separation has barely developed. His apposition of the baby doll to the mother doll fits this, as does his putting the baby doll under his jumper. His play with the dolls is very meaningful. My reason for not taking it up directly is that he uses it defensively to draw me into treating him as even younger and less able than he is. This begs the question of whether it is useful to provide such toys to an adolescent patient.

The father's role is interesting. I believe I become the father in the transference when I speak particularly in a way that breaks the safe routine, and this is most vivid when I bring his curiosity to his attention. At this point he projects his curiosity into me so that it becomes a dangerous attribute of his father, but as such is less dangerous than being an attribute of his own or his mother's. Although he is frightened of his father, he mentions his father more often and with more enthusiasm than he mentions his mother; I suspect that he has a split view of his father, so that, on the one hand his father is more dangerous, and on the other hand more benign, than his mother, who is protected from curiosity, both his and her own. When I interpret his fear, following the telephone call, I am experienced by him in a paternal position that is more benign, and he then experiences curiosity as less dangerous.

Sam's material illustrates a common propensity in people with learning disabilities to feel bound to fit in with a view of themselves that originates in their parents' minds as handicapped but perpetually child-like, in some way perfect, even gifted. In this state, curiosity and knowledge are prohibited.

In more recent work with Sam, I became aware of how, when faced with change, he would retreat into a more regressed and handicapped state: for example, making frequent demands for the toilet. I think he found being like a handicapped child much easier than showing a more age-appropriate adolescent self of which I saw signs but from which he would quickly retreat. The very situation of being brought to the therapy at the request of his teachers embodied this problem. Although he genuinely wanted to come, he was also complying with what he perceived to be other people's need for him to come, including mine. Towards the end of our work, I saw more genuine protest about this from him, which I viewed as progress.

To return to the use of the term "learning disability": I think that those who have sought to do away with specific diagnosis and bring a multitude of problems under this umbrella term have laid the way for further problems in their attempts to remove stigmatization. The defensive constellation that Sam illustrates of taking refuge in a state of perpetual childhood, for which the price is additional handicap, is a common phenomenon. The danger in using the term "learning disability", which obscures a distinction between organic and psychological deficits, is that it can so easily fit in with this. In so doing, it can become a refuge for all concerned, including professionals, from really knowing a person's capacities and incapacities and from where they might derive: a refuge where both capability and incapability can hide. Its origin lies in our difficulties in giving up our illusions and facing how things really are.

CHAPTER SIX

Adolescents with learning disabilities: psychic structures that are not conducive to learning

Lynda Miller

In this chapter I discuss what I have come to feel is a significant factor in the psychotherapeutic treatment of some young people with learning disabilities. It is a factor that can affect the nature of the transference relationship in a negative way. If it is not understood and interpreted by the therapist, it can impede the patient's capacity to learn through experience from the process of therapy itself. If the therapist is felt by the patient to have a secretly harsh, critical, or judgemental attitude towards those with learning disabilities, the patient will tend to placate the therapist or conform to what he or she feels is being expected in a self-protective or defensive manner.

I suggest that this kind of relationship, highly detrimental to learning, in which a harsh critical figure is projected into the therapist in the transference relationship, originates in early infancy in the primary pre-oedipal relationship between the baby and the mother.

This chapter has previously appeared in the *Journal of Child Psychotherapy*, 28 (2002, no. 1). The Journal's website can be found at <www.tandf.co.uk>.

When parents give birth to a baby with a visible disability such as Down's syndrome, shock and disappointment may be reflected in their eyes, even if they are attempting to conceal or to overcome these powerful emotions. In a recent paper called "Relating to the Super-Ego", Edna O'Shaughnessy (1999), a contemporary Kleinian analyst and writer, discusses Bion's (1967b) concept of the ego-destructive superego. She refers to a psychic condition that can contribute to the formation of an abnormal superego: that of "an abnormal state of mind in the mother condemning the baby for not matching her anticipated ideal".

One could argue that all parents have a preconception of an ideal baby, a baby that is different from the real baby to which they give birth. I would like to suggest that in the case of a baby born with a visible learning disability—that is, in cases where it is accompanied by or integral to physical manifestations of disability—this difference is so acute as to have a potentially traumatic effect upon the infant–parent relationship. An infant who experiences himself through what he perceives in his parents' eyes as they look at him as being not the child they wanted will internalize this perception. This may generate the formation of a harshly judgemental superego. The superego can be understood as the function of self-reflective consciousness. A harsh superego judges and usurps the ego and looks upon the self with critical eyes, and in the case of a baby with a learning disability there may be an internalization of the eyes of the parents who look at their infant with emotions clouded by disappointment, still having in mind the anticipated perfect baby with whom they unconsciously wish to replace their real but damaged baby. In Bion's (1967b) view, such a serious disturbance arises not solely from an internalization of the infant's perception of parental hostility, but from a primitive yet complex interplay between self and object, in which the infant's own aggressive impulses play a part. Thus, constitutionally some infants may be more prone to developing severe emotional difficulties in life than others.

The formation of a harsh and judgemental superego will generate the very low self-esteem that one often finds when working therapeutically with learning-disabled adolescents. It is this powerfully negative view of themselves that leads learning-disabled adolescents to readily take on their societal role as excluded, unwanted outsiders, preferably remaining unseen by others. It may also impede their capacities to develop and to learn because the fundamental sense of self is damaged and is felt to be incapable of healthy cognitive growth.

In a clinical setting, such patients may feel that they are "all wrong" for therapy, "too stupid" to engage in the therapeutic process, or not entitled to participate in a process that, they may feel, belongs to the non-learning-disabled world. An 18-year-old young man began all of his early sessions by telling me that his mum says he does not have to come to the Clinic if he does not like it. In this, and in many other ways, he himself would undermine his commitment to attending his psychotherapy sessions by not taking his own needs seriously. I felt that he was convinced that I saw him as an unsuitable patient for treatment—as if he were a much younger boy who did not have a mind of his own and could not make his own decision about his treatment. Fortunately, through a careful exploration of these feelings, he has continued to attend his sessions and to make good use of psychotherapy.

Clinical material

"Elaine"

Elaine[1] is an 18-year-old young woman of Afro–Caribbean origin who had been assessed and for whom individual psychotherapy had been recommended. She lives with her mother, who is a single parent. I began to see Elaine for once-weekly psychotherapy, but I was quickly to become acquainted with a difficult and painful issue that most learning-disabled adolescents have to contend with regarding attending the Clinic for therapy: that of their wish to be independent of parents or carers, in an age-appropriate way, being offset against the problem of managing to travel to and from the Clinic on their own.

For Elaine (who could travel by herself on public transport despite finding money difficult to manage) this was far less difficult than for many learning-disabled patients who have to be escorted, yet it still became a major stumbling-block.

An extract from Elaine's first therapy session follows:

Elaine arrived 10 minutes early. Her manner was friendly but guarded and anxious, and she was carefully dressed and made up. She spoke immediately of the problem of coming to the Clinic, because she had to travel on the tube, with little time to spare to fit in with her college timetable. She then talked of how tense she had been when she saw Mrs B for the assessment and how anxious she is in all situations: if she goes out, she tenses up and hyper-ventilates and expects people to say things about her.

I talked about her coming to see me today: the difficulties of the journey, her worries about what I will say, and that despite these anxieties she has managed to come here. She spoke again of the problem of her timetable, and we worked out a change of time for therapy that might be more manageable. She said this was fine. I felt retrospectively that she had been over-accommodating.

She then talked about her two main problems: first, wanting to disappear, for nobody to see her, and, second, being obsessed with dieting, a fear of being fat. I said that perhaps there is a connection between her two problems. I linked her wish to disappear with her wish to be thin, as if there is something about herself that she wants no one to see and to know about. She talked of a fear of being fat, of seeing fat people in magazines and dreading that is how she will be seen. I talked to her of her possible worries about how she feels I will see her and explained that this is something we can try to understand together. I added that she is perhaps feeling that I will have unkind thoughts in my mind.

She flushed and said that other children have always called her names, right through all her schools. She gave a long, painful account of this, beginning with nursery school, when a teacher told her that she must learn the alphabet, and she couldn't. She then got behind with all her school work, seeing the other children able to do it, and they called her names. She felt so different from the other children. At her next school it was worse, so she stayed home and had a tutor for two years, which was very lonely. She wanted to go back to school, but she was too frightened of being bullied. Eventually she told her mum that she wanted to go back to school, but not to that one, so her mum found her a new school.

I talked about a strong part of her that wanted to go back to school to be with other children, despite her fears, and it is this part that has brought her here today. She wants to grow and to develop—not to feel badly about herself, and afraid of what others are thinking about her, as if she feels that she is very different from them. She seems to feel that her learning problems are visible to all, like being fat, and she wants to get rid of this part of herself, for it to disappear.

She said she wants to go out and be a normal teenager. She is obsessed with dieting and can't eat lunch, even though she feels weak in the afternoons. She described her mum as overweight and always trying to make her eat more. We talked about her mixed feelings towards food, and perhaps towards therapy; of her knowing that this is something she needs, yet her fear that this is being forced upon her.

We agreed that we would continue meeting but at a different time that she could manage more easily; however, gradually I found myself feeling uncomfortable in the sessions that followed, and I became aware of a split transference—her overt relationship with me as a helpful and friendly person, yet her unspoken fear that I was privately critical of her. I had a sense that this corresponded to a harsh and judgemental superego and that Elaine readily felt that others were having negative thoughts about her.

After some weeks Elaine's mother telephoned me to say that Elaine was very upset because the journey to the Clinic, and then on to college, is too complicated for her. She panics and goes home after sessions, missing a whole day of college each week. Elaine had not felt able to tell me this. In the next session, it was possible to face with her the conflicts involved for her in coming to the Clinic. Her old situation had been revived at college: she had to have extra help to make up for the time she lost on the day she attended her session, and this made her feel upset and confused—yet again, behind with her work and different from all the other students. She was ashamed to tell me this, and the session was painful but useful as we worked together in differentiating her anxieties from the reality of her situation. It was then possible to make an arrangement for a different day, when she did not attend college. Elaine became able to allow herself to have opportunities to learn in different ways by attending both college and therapy.

Her conscious desire to be part of ordinary college life had been undermined by the harsh and judgemental part of herself that had prevented her from being able to talk to me openly about her travelling difficulty, as if anticipating that I would be critical and unsympathetic about her learning disability. This point is in accord with Valerie Sinason's (1992b) concept of "secondary handicap" whereby emotional factors add another dimension to the original learning disability, with the effect of exaggerating the handicap. Sinason (1992b, p. 2) wrote: "the primary handicap (or disability) is made worse by defensive exaggerations (secondary handicap). For some of us, an area of disability is particularly vulnerable to the most damaging secondary handicapping processes."

"Rose"

My second clinical example is that of Rose, aged 19 years. She was referred to our service by her social worker because she would stay in her own room watching television for much of the daytime and all of the evening. Rose has a moderate learning disability and a speech impediment. She looks and dresses as if she were much younger than her actual age. Her social worker described to us her concerns about Rose's inability to manage social situations. She was frightened to leave her house or, indeed, to go anywhere by herself, or to participate in social gatherings of any kind. She suffered from panic attacks when faced with new situations and was generally highly anxious.

PSYCHIC STRUCTURES NOT CONDUCIVE TO LEARNING

Rose had, however, said to her social worker that she would like to talk to someone who would help her with her difficulties. She has been living with her foster parents since she was 6 years old. They had hoped that Rose would become more sociable when she became a teenager, but this had not been the case.

I had seen Rose for six assessment sessions to which she had been brought by her foster mother. Rose has a good relationship with her foster parents, who have three younger children of their own. They have tried with Rose's social worker to encourage Rose to mix with other people of her own age, but with no success. Rose prefers to watch television in her own room, although she would sometimes play with her foster parents' youngest daughter, aged 5 years, with enjoyment.

She was very anxious throughout the assessment, and at times her speech was extremely difficult to understand. However, I found that if I relaxed and just listened rather than straining to decode every word, I became increasingly able to understand what she was saying, and, correspondingly, Rose's anxiety gradually lessened.

Despite her obvious fears about talking to me, an unknown person, and her worries that I would not be able to comprehend her communications, I sensed an underlying determination in Rose to overcome her anxieties about attending the Clinic, and to commit herself to coming regularly for therapy.

Here is an extract from Rose's first therapy session:

I heard from ground-floor reception that Rose had arrived for her session, and I asked that she should be directed to the waiting-room on the third floor (in accordance with her appointment letter). When she did not arrive, I waited by the lifts, then heard Rose's voice coming from the second floor, asking how to get to the third floor, and having to repeat her question because of her speech difficulty.

She came up the stairs, and on the way to my room talked about asking someone for help, and they told her where to go. I felt that Rose wanted me to see her as having managed to get to the third floor by herself, not as someone who had got lost. In the therapy-room I talked with Rose about the arrangements for the therapy, and I said that we would have holiday breaks. Rose was silent, looking at me searchingly. She then said in a clear voice, "I go on holiday in November." I said I thought Rose had thought about what I had said and is telling me that she is also taking a holiday, but that she can come back for therapy after that, too. She said anxiously, "Tell Jane and Joe."

I said that we will make sure that all the arrangements are clear, but Rose perhaps gets anxious and feels she will not be able to remember dates. I referred to my letter to Rose giving her the appointment day today, and she is here.

Rose said, "Jane told me" and "Joe told me". We clarified that her foster parents had read my letter to Rose, and that in fact I had written to them too. Rose then mentioned the names of the older two children in her foster family and said that sometimes they come into her room now and talk to her, and this was said with a proud smile. Then she said that she stays in her room by herself and watches television.

I said that Rose and I had talked a lot during her assessment about how she stays in her room by herself. Although she still does so, she is letting me know of a change. She is pleased that now people come in her room and talk to her. This perhaps joins up with her feelings about coming here—her coming up to my room and talking to me. In a way it is easier for her to shut herself in her own room, but Rose now wants more in her life than this. She can manage to talk with me, and she has come today to begin her therapy, to talk with me every week, even though she needs the help of Jane and Joe to read my letters to her.

Rose then told me that she had come by herself today. She said that she had got a bit panicked: it is a long way and she had to take two trains. Jane and Joe told her to phone if she gets lost, and she has the phone number and address of the Clinic. I said that is a big change for Rose. I think that she is letting me know that she has strong feelings about her therapy—this is something she is doing for herself, and she is determined to come here by herself. Rose smiled and then frowned. She said, "What do you mean?" I said I thought Rose had understood me, but she is not used to thinking about herself in this way—strong and determined. She came by herself even though she panicked a bit. Rose smiled with shining eyes and said, "Trains are different from buses." She paused and said "brave", with a questioning look at me. I said Rose wants to know that I understand that it is important to her, and that she has been brave— a big step.

Rose said, "Jane said be careful." I said Rose has told me this before. She knows she does need to be careful, but this does not need to stop her from talking to people, coming to therapy, travelling alone.

Rose then talked about Jane being upset. She told me a story about a woman who had knocked at the door and asked for a glass of water, then had stolen Jane's bag.

I thought about the transference implications of this, of Rose's fear and mistrust of me; but I felt that an interpretation of this kind might be confusing for Rose. As a psychotherapist working with young people with learning disabilities, I feel that there are a number of issues about technique that can usefully be discussed. It seems important to me to maintain a focus upon the relationship that the young person makes with the therapist—in other words, to study the transference and the countertransference and to interpret accordingly, but at the same time to take care that transference interpretations are not received as statements of fact. I think that if I had suggested to Rose that there could be a link in her mind between this intrusive, untrustworthy woman and her fears about me, her therapist, I would only have caused her confusion. To return to the session, Rose said again that Jane was upset and looked sad. I said, "The woman played a trick", and Rose said, "Yes". I said I thought Rose tells herself to be careful and that she does have different sorts of feelings about coming to talk with me, about beginning therapy today: perhaps it is hard for her to feel she can trust me. I said we can try to understand Rose's thoughts and feelings when we meet together for her sessions. She is used to keeping all this private. It is a big change for her.

It was then time to stop, and I accompanied Rose to the lift. She looked unsure what to do and laughed anxiously. I indicated the button to press and Rose said, "Sorry, sorry", in an anxious, apologetic way.

This had been an expression she had used frequently throughout the assessment. I have been struck by the placatory quality of her misplaced apologies. At one level it is as if she blames herself for anything that goes wrong on the basis that it could not be my fault, it must be hers, as she is learning disabled. However, my countertransference experience of receiving her apologies is very uncomfortable. I think, as in the case of Elaine, it implies an internal object-relationship in Rose's mind characterized by a harsh and judgemental superego figure, which is projected into me in the transference relationship. This figure is not helpful and friendly towards Rose but, like the tricky woman who steals Jane's bag, is intent upon stealing something from Rose: the confidence and independence which she wants so much to develop.

However, after one year of therapy, Rose was able to recognize in herself the way in which she kept putting herself down, almost apologizing for her existence. Whenever she caught herself saying "sorry" to me in an inappropriate context, she would laugh in acknowledgement. After two years of therapy, she was much more able to speak up for herself, no longer needing to placate this harsh superego figure that had been projected into me in the transference and had kept her in a fearful and isolated state. She had learned to relate to me in the therapy, and to others in her external world, in a more realistic way. This enabled her to learn from others: to feel that she was worthy of receiving help and that she would make good use of it. She increased her attendance at college, and moved into a house for learning-disabled young people in which they had live-in workers to help them but also had a considerable degree of independence.

In a session a few months before the agreed ending date of the therapy, I noted that Rose's speech was becoming clearer and also that at times in the sessions she was less placatory, less "nice". She reported in a somewhat defiant manner that she had told her social worker that she had "done well" at therapy so she did not need to attend any longer. She let me know that the social worker said, "do what you want", so that is what she is going to do. She then told me that she likes her new house because "you do not need to lock your bedroom door, people don't break in and steal things".

These comments by Rose led me to feel that she is more able to experience her own sense of value, as well as her own aggression, and that her ego is strengthened as a result of the therapeutic process. She is much less dominated by a harsh superego in her relationship with me, and I have a sense that she had taken into herself qualities of strength and resilience.

"Beatrice"

For my third clinical illustration, I am grateful to one of my colleagues for contributing material on the following patient, whom I heard about in supervision.

Beatrice is a 17-year-old young woman with Down's syndrome. Her appearance is rather unkempt, and she dresses in old-fashioned clothes and shoes, which make her look more like a little girl than an adolescent. She has recently moved into a hostel for young people with learning disabilities, and was referred to the Clinic by her keyworker, who felt that Beatrice was depressed. She stays with her family at weekends, and they too were concerned about their daughter. Beatrice had not wanted to attend College, and they thought that she was not developing to her full potential.

The therapist described her work with this patient as follows:

In early sessions, Beatrice would often give the impression that she was dragged to the Clinic by her keyworker against her will. She spoke of missing a TV programme that was on at the time of the session, she would look away from her therapist, and she had a hostile attitude. It seemed extremely difficult for her to think that her therapist could be interested in her, and she would constantly ask in a defensive way questions like "Is there anything else you want to say to me?" or "Is there anything else you want to know?"—as though the answer in her mind could only be negative. Interpretations of these feelings seemed to have no effect. However, when the therapist did ask her a direct question about any aspect of her life, she would start talking, relating loosely connected incidents from her life without pausing and in a flat tone of voice.

In the sessions that followed it became clear that Beatrice felt cut off from the world, as if there is no place for her in any relationship. She seemed to feel as if she was completely isolated from other young people of her age, who, she said, could "go out after dark" or "talk on the phone for hours". Her desperate need to make a link was manifest in an obsessive collection of phone numbers, addresses, and photographs of people she knew—as if relationships could not exist in her mind without this concrete evidence. In the transference the therapist could see that she desperately wanted to make a link with her, but at the same time she would attack this link. There were moments of real communication, which were usually followed by Beatrice trying to turn the session into a game, mimicking the therapist's gestures and laughing at her. She talked about having the therapist's phone number and being able to leave a message for her, but when she said she would phone her, it was said in a way that suggested that she thought this would only be a nuisance to her therapist. She seemed to fear that the therapist would not want to see her again and she often asked about this at the end of the session. She seemed unable to believe that a relationship could be sustained in which the participants are genuinely interested in each other.

Beatrice often said that she did not like change, and she seemed to be immobilized in a frozen state—neither a child nor an adolescent. She was aware of how bodies change in adolescence but seemed confused about her identity as a young woman.

Beatrice communicates feelings of depression and extreme hopelessness, linked to her voiced thought that she has "no future". She talks about other people urging her to get a life "out of the house", but she seems paralysed by a difficulty in thinking for herself and an inability to decide what she wants. In one session she talked about "people out there who have different religions and like different things". She said that everybody has a life, but she herself is not sure about what she really wants. She asked the therapist if she could help her get a life, and the therapist tried to explore with her what getting a life a would mean for her. She said it was "having thoughts about the world outside", and "like when I close my mind, I can still see you". The therapist said that Beatrice was now beginning to have an image of her in her mind, and she reported the following interchanges. Beatrice asked "Can *you* think in your mind?" and the therapist said that she was wondering whether she could keep Beatrice in her mind and think about her. At the end of this session Beatrice said, "Today we talked about having thoughts."

I think this material gives a clear illustration of the thawing of Beatrice's frozen state of mind, described so carefully by her therapist.

Beatrice becomes able to use her mind as her intelligence is mobilized in the process of the therapeutic relationship. Her ego is strengthened, and through the positive link that has developed with her therapist, Beatrice begins to experience herself as a person who can have her own life in the world outside. She seems to be saying that first she needs to be able to imagine herself in this way, to have thoughts in her mind about the world outside and herself in it, and she feels that her therapist will be able to help her with this, with her thinking mind. Her harsh superego, which makes her feel like a child isolated and stuck in a stagnant childhood, is gradually modified by the relationship with her therapist, who offers understanding and empathy rather than the negative and critical attitude anticipated by Beatrice.

Discussion

Bion (1962a) described patients who suffer from disordered and distorted thinking processes. He used the abstract term "–K" to denote the reversal of the K function, I would like to suggest that a relationship characterized by –K can be typified by an internal harsh superego in relation to an ego depleted of the capacity to think. Bion states that K (which stands for knowledge, or the desire to know) is essentially a function of two objects, at source the projections of an infant's emotional states of mind into the mind of its mother. Bion writes of these projections: "During their sojourn in the good breast they are felt to have been modified in such a way that the object that is re-introjected has become tolerable to the infant's psyche."

Bion uses the term "contained" to refer to the projected mental states of the infant and "the container" to refer to the mother's receptive state of mind or in the language of early infantile experience, the good breast. This shared two-way communication is mutually beneficial to mother and to baby and leads to the emotional and cognitive development of the infant.

For Bion, "–K" refers to the reversal of this process. Negative factors in the minds of infant or mother can generate a relationship that is antagonistic to mental growth. In healthy cognitive development, when there is a K-link between mother and infant, the latter introjects the container–contained relationship. The predominant quality of the superego relationship to the ego—the internalization of the mother–infant K-link—is benign and conducive to the development of thinking. The reversal of this process, when the mother–infant relationship is characterized by "–K", generates a superego formation that has particular qualities. Bion writes that it "shows itself as a superior object asserting its superiority by finding fault with everything. The most important characteristic is its hatred of any new development in the personality as if the new development were a rival to be destroyed. The emergence therefore of any tendency to search for the truth, to establish contact with reality ... is met by destructive attacks on the tendency" (p. 98). I would like to suggest that when Beatrice attacks links with her therapist by mimicking and laughing at her, she's exemplifying a "–K" relationship with her therapist.

I think that for learning-disabled adolescents this can be understood in the context of the parent–infant relationship that I described at the beginning of this chapter: one in which the shock and disappointment that may be inherent in the parents' experience of giving birth to a visibly disabled infant serves as a negative factor for the infant in the process of internalizing the container–contained psychic formation that enables thinking to be generated. In cases where the learning disability becomes apparent in childhood rather than in infancy, social attitudes towards disability have a considerable contribution to make in terms of generating very low self-esteem in learning-disabled people.

A harsh and critical superego does not allow the learning-disabled child to develop to full potential. Organic damage or genetic syndrome certainly limit some aspects of cognitive functioning, sometimes severely so, but in psychotherapeutic work with learning-disabled patients it frequently becomes apparent that there are other factors that work against growth and development. One of these factors is an internal voice, that of the ego-destructive superego, which constantly reminds the learning-disabled person at an unconscious level that he or she is not the child the parents wished to know. This implies exclusion from the world of human relationships, because for the infant the parents are the whole world. This relationship is internalized and then projected into all other subsequent relationships.

It can be projected into the therapist by the patient—hence the discomfort of the countertransference experience. But the therapist is in a position to observe this relationship as it unfolds, to help the patient to see what is happening, and, if the therapy proceeds well, to modify this harsh and distorted link into one that is more conducive to the development of thinking.

Note

1. An extended version of the material on the patient I have called "Elaine" appears in a chapter entitled "Psychotherapy with Learning Disabled Adolescents", in R. Anderson and A. Dartington (Eds.), *Facing It Out* (London: Duckworth, 1998).

CHAPTER SEVEN

The creative use of limited language in psychotherapy by an adolescent with a severe learning disability

Annie Baikie

This chapter is about language and about loss, about thinking and about attacks on thinking, about challenge, and about development.
Individual psychotherapy involves two people—the patient and the psychotherapist—and for the therapy to have a positive impact upon the patient, both parties have to have access to learning. In psychotherapy this learning has to co-exist in a particular way, the psychotherapist getting to know the patient and the patient getting to understand him or herself within the context of that relationship. This is what Bion (1962a) called K, an attempt on the therapist's part to understand the patient, to get to know the patient, not by an accumulation of theoretical concepts but by an intimate process of knowing, which may or may not be achieved. In therapeutic work with patients with learning disabilities many complex issues become entangled between patient and psychotherapist.
Valerie Sinason (1992b) has written about "secondary handicap": she writes that in thinking about the nature of attacks on intelligent thinking, we give people with learning disabilities the

opportunity not to be stupid, and although people with learning disabilities might never be able to do certain things that we take for granted, they still need the emotional loan of these things.

In this chapter I talk about my patient "Buna", what I believe was the major factor impeding her learning, and what could have been the major factor impeding my learning, had it not been for Buna's remarkable and creative use of her very limited language.

But first I would like to tell you a story:

Some years ago I went to a party; the majority of the guests were analysts and psychotherapists. In each room small groups of people were "talking shop". However, I found myself watching the way the non-therapists—a small band of partners and old friends—interacted. There appeared to be three groups within that category of non-therapists. Group number 1 was the obviously interested; group number 2 was feigning interest; and then there was group number 3. Now, this group seemed articulate, thoughtful, and somewhat cunning. They seemed to be using all their linguistic powers to ask interesting questions, all of which appeared to have the sole purpose of tripping up the person on the receiving end.

I found myself mesmerized by a particular guest who was questioning a psychotherapist. My anxiety rose as the questioner began talking about research and statistics: *"I'm not asking for statistics, but can you name the three commonest problems people come to see you with?"* asked the questioner. I gazed at the woman who was about to answer, wondering what on earth she was going to say. She smiled slightly and said, *"Oh! that's easy, everyone always come with the same thing—loss—it just comes in different guises."* It's funny how, whatever we think we have learnt, whatever we think we know, something can be said, and it just makes such sense.

"Buna"

Buna's whole life seemed to be about loss. She was born in Northern Ireland in 1982. She was born with Down's syndrome, and as she developed, it was clear that she had severe learning disabilities. In 1992, when she was 10, her father died and her brother attempted suicide and was hospitalized. In 1994 Buna, her mother, sister, and brother moved to Leicester. Her mother and brother were both very depressed. Just before the move to Leicester, Mrs S took Buna to their country of origin, where Buna had a hysterectomy. She was 11.

Shortly after moving to Leicester, at her mother's request, Buna was accommodated in a small group home. Mother has had sporadic contact with Buna. She frequently travels to her country of origin for long periods, sometimes eight months at a time, without warning. Buna has regular contact with her sister and brother, and during this contact she sometimes sees her mother. Throughout her time in the group home, Buna has presented problems: aggressiveness, swearing, inappropriate behaviours that were difficult for her carers to manage; it would be fair to say that she was deemed to have challenging behaviour.

After an initial settling-in period at the group home, the staff asked the local community learning disability team for help. The psychologists in the team worked with Buna, the staff at the home, and within the school setting. This involved a lot of talking and a lot of thinking about Buna's behaviour, monitoring her behaviour and setting up a structured programme of activities in order to offer more stability and consistency in her life. It was all to have a positive result. One of the most interesting aspects of the community learning disability team's work was that the staff filled in a form recording their own perspective of Buna's experiences and emotions and were given opportunities to discuss them on a regular basis with someone from the team. In doing this, they too began to feel understood and therefore to have access to understanding Buna. Both the community learning disability team and the workers in the group home felt that through the success of this work, Buna should go on to receive individual therapy, and a referral was made to the Learning Disabilities Service at the Tavistock Clinic.

One of the members of the service saw Buna for an assessment. She was seen six times over a period of three months, and it was thought that she would be a suitable candidate for therapy. I then began to see her for long-term once-weekly individual psychotherapy.

In retrospect, a number of things occur to me about both the referral and the assessment. Within the referral, there was a concern about her very limited language, and the question came up as to whether the therapist would "know Makaton". This seems rather ironic now, considering that Buna only once used a Makaton[1] sign within her therapy, and, indeed, she seemed to have no need for sign language as a means of communication, due to the powerful emotional content that was conveyed to me through her, albeit limited, verbal language.

Buna was very quick to use language to express what was happening within the therapeutic relationship.

In the corridor before her second psychotherapy session she refused to come with me. The workers struggled to deal with this, having to manage Buna as well as their own fears and anxieties at this first hurdle. "Don't like" said Buna when they tried to cajole her. Once in the room, most of the session was taken up with spitting, teeth grinding, making faces, and the words "cow" and "pig", and "sorry".

I tried to describe what was going on and how she might be feeling and how she wanted to make me feel. When I paused from speaking, she looked at me and said, "talk". I had no doubt from the tone and from the way she looked at me that she was not asking me to simply fill the time with my words, but that she was inviting me to understand and make sense of what she brought.

Over the first six months of treatment I began to learn Buna's language—the way that "pig" and "cow" could refer to how bad she felt about herself. But it could also be used to express her anger and frustration when I did not understand what she said or I made an interpretation that was way off mark and, most of all, when she could not be bothered: at those times there was no doubt that the "cow" or "pig" were aimed firmly at me. She also used them to show affection for me, describing the warmth that had developed between us and the playfulness that warmth could lend to her words, looking up at me with a shy smile saying, "How now brown cow".

In an early session, when I first used the word "stupid" about how I thought she felt and also how she wanted people to see her, she looked across at me and said, very quickly, "Peter Piper picked a peck of pickled pepper, the pepper Peter Piper picked" and she broke off and looked at me. I thought with her about her determination to show me that she was clever and that she had intelligent thinking.

There was a great deal of "sorrys": sorry to me, sorry to mum, sorry to staff, school friends, and people she lived with. She demanded "juice" and "sweets" incessantly—taking my interpretations that the food I had for her were my words with great disdain. "Cry" she demanded both of herself and me. It felt impossible for her to cry, although she felt so sad.

In the first five months, much of her speech was repetitious, as were the sounds she made. At first I picked through what I thought were the most relevant, but gradually I tuned in to listen and watch more carefully, however soporific it felt. I began to wonder if sometimes I simply made interpretations to keep myself awake. If she made noises or sounds, I would not just comment, I would imitate or join in, rhyming, 1, 2, ... clapping or tapping, anything to keep me in the conversation. These were techniques I was familiar with both in my drama therapy work and in using interactive therapy in special education. With Buna I would join in with her echolalia. Buna found it both amusing and interesting. She would give me much greater eye contact and became much more focused. I would not need to keep it up very long; it had its own development, which was both playful and creative and served as a way for both of us to be reconnected to the other.

Maria Rhode (1999) writes about echolalia as "the move towards ordinary speech". Buna's echo took in what I said and what she said and connected us. Thinking of Buna's use of language in this way reminds me of the playful quality of her words. However, they also mirrored much darker, more painful moments. In the past Buna had received many harsh reprimands and painful words, and these were stuck inside her. Like a broken record, they added to her sense of guilt, and the many "sorrys" were not always about warding off any punitive or aggressive feelings but simply answering words stuck in her mind.

Buna continued to come, the staff who escorted her becoming less anxious that she would hit a child in the waiting-room. They began to sit with her in the waiting-room rather than hovering nervously in the corridor. She became known among the reception staff both upstairs and down, and with the patients and carers who came at the same time. She would shout, to make her arrival known, and also shout, "*BAIKIE!*", leaving no doubt whom she had come to see. For a long time she would only come to the room if Bob, one of the workers, would come with her to the door. This appeared at first to be a helpful transition, the coming and going being difficult. Then it appeared to turn into something more amusing for her, and she seemed keen to make a connection between Bob and me—perhaps her idealized parental couple.

Her language developed: more words were used, and through her experience of taking in my interpretations, she seemed to find more and more creative ways to communicate that she understood an idea. In Session 15, after two missed appointments, she was visibly shaking in the corridor with anger and refusing to come into the waiting-room or with me. The staff accompanying her were surprised, telling me, "she wants to come, she has been saying your name, asking for you for three weeks". Buna looked up at me and said, "Too hard—no go." Eventually she came to the room, helped by her very thoughtful workers. I made an interpretation about the difficult feelings stirred up by the two missed sessions. Though it appeared that she took no notice, at the end of the session, as I opened the door, she said, "Sorry Baikie".

During Session 22 I felt that the words that Buna had been bringing over the past six months came together as a story, and this marked a real move in the therapy.

> She started the session by telling me that there was a fight at the club she attends. "Peregrine fight—hurt me. Boy hurt me." I am surprised by these different words she was able to use.
>
> "Buna hurts, Buna hurts." She pointed to her neck and said, "hurt neck". I said that she is telling me that she had a fight and that she got hurt; that her neck hurts but also her feelings are hurt. In between she nodded, saying, "hurt . . . Buna hurt".
>
> I suggested to her that she was telling me about different types of hurts: hurts on the neck and hurts inside. She said, "Mummy,

Daddy, swear at Mummy, Daddy, bad girl no swear." I said that she has lots of different feelings. She looked very sad. I thought that perhaps she feels very sad when she thinks about her mum and dad, sad that they do not like her swearing, sad that they might think Buna was bad, and perhaps she wonders, what I will think? "No swear", she said angrily. I said that she also had very angry feelings about mum and dad, about school, and about me. She comes all this way to the Tavistock Clinic to see Annie Baikie, where there appears to be no treats, no juice, no chips, but a place where all her sad and angry feelings come out. She started spitting—but very slightly, more making the noise for dramatic effect—and I said, "You are reminding me just how angry you can be with me and you are spitting at me just to let me know what you think of me." "Cow", she said.

She looked up at me; she tried to cry, squeezing her eyes. Her presence felt very sad, and she was unusually still. In a desperately sad voice, she said, "Daddy sorry", "Sorry Daddy", "Sorry swear Daddy", " Daddy", "Buna did it, yes" "Buna did it", "Daddy died".

I said that she is so sorry about Daddy and worried that she hurt Daddy, hurt his feelings, or that she hurt him so much with her words that she killed him. It is very sad that Buna's Daddy has died, sad for Buna that she doesn't have her Daddy any more but sad about the events that happened after her Daddy died, that Mummy felt so sad about her Daddy's death that she could not look after Buna any more and Buna had to go and live in another place away from her Mummy. It's hard for Buna to believe that Mummy didn't send her away because she thought Buna hurt Daddy and part of Buna feels so angry that Mummy sent her away because part of Buna knows that she didn't hurt Daddy. "Say it again" she said loudly. I said it again, saying that she really wanted to hear.

Buna said quietly, "Baby, baby is here". She then looked very odd, as if she did not know whether to laugh or cry. I said that Buna is letting me know that she brings here a very baby part of her, a very small part of her, and that I need to be very careful with that baby and look after it. "You're funny", she said, smiling at me.

After this session there did seem to be more understanding between us: the spitting disappeared and stayed away for a year. In terms of her language it was as if she opened a box of words and phrases, songs and rhymes that she had locked away. Now she was using them to make a link with me. She seemed to say, "This is all I have, but I will make it work between us."

When I brought up the Christmas break, a two-week gap in her therapy, she started singing, "Oh I do like to be beside the seaside" (a song about holidays) linking her idea of holidays with mine. Her language continued to develop, and her normal plea of "cry" turned into a question: "How do you cry?", and her "help" into a request: "Help with crying." The session after the Christmas break she came back, furious.

"Annie Pig, Pig Baikie hurt Buna. Annie hurt Buna". After I made an interpretation of being left, feeling abandoned, she said, "See-saw", "up–down", "back–forward".

I said that she felt that she was on a see-saw with me, that her feelings are like a see-saw.

Buna began asking me to "talk". She moved into "say it again" and then to "tell". If I made an interpretation that seemed to take a real hold of her, she would ask me to tell, tell the workers and then, even more strongly, "tell Mummy". When she said to me, "tell Mummy, Buna sad" I felt that there needed to be something more than an interpretation. I picked up a piece of paper out of her box and wrote:

Dear Mrs Z, Buna has asked me to tell you that she is very sad and when she thinks about you and her Daddy she is so sad that she can't cry. She is so full of sadness that if she started to cry she thinks she would not be able to stop."

I read it out to her. She said, "again". Now we have two more additions to our work, "write" and "read it". Buna's box became full of writing, and it was clear how important our words written down were to her.

I developed this idea of using writing as part of the therapy from Judith Usiskin and Jenny Sprince (both child psychotherapists), who ran a therapeutic group at the Tavistock Clinic for women with learning disabilities. Each week the therapist took responsibility for writing down what the group members said, and this was distributed to the women the following week. When presenting this work, Jenny Sprince and Judith Usiskin commented: "How concretely the women experienced the containment we offered through this writing process. It becomes clear that having their words written down, a concrete form of being listened to, had a quite physical meaning for them, which is the same as warmth and food" (personal communication, and in Sinason, 1992b).

Buna stopped asking for juice and sweets once the writing started.

As Easter approached, Buna let me know that the break was on her mind and what she felt about it.

> "Hot cross buns,
> One a penny,
> Two a penny,
> Hot cross buns."

Then (to the tune of the song *London's Burning*), from seemingly nowhere came

> "Buna's burning, Buna's burning,
> She is angry, she is angry."

Then she said, "want mama", and sang, "want mama, want mama". I responded that she was not able to tell her Mummy, only Annie. There was a pause, she made some noises, some teeth grinding, and then she sang (again to the tune of *London's Burning*),

> "Buna's burning, Buna's burning,
> She is angry, she is angry,
> wants mama, mama, only tell Annie."

I was so struck by what she had done that there was a moment of absolute stillness. I sang it back to her, and after the first "Buna's burning" she joined in with me.

For her review meeting, she gave me, albeit in her own way, a list of things to share with the group manager.

THE CREATIVE USE OF LIMITED LANGUAGE   107

1. "You and me."
2. "I feel sorry."
3. "I want to cry."
4. "If I'm silly, try again."
5. "Not sorry for some things."
6. "Try again, Mama."

At the meeting I found that the workers felt that there had been an enormous change in her. The manager shyly told me, "You know, she was very difficult to like. We worked very hard at it, and we managed it, but now we really like her, and it feels so different. We feel we understand her far more."

With more thoughts and more interpretations, the language altered around the principal words of her vocabulary. Rather than the repetition of single words, such as "Sorry, cry, spit", she began to join the words into long sentences—for instance, "I cry and I cry again, hurt the baby, baby cry, alright Mummy, sorry Mummy, try again, I try again, Mummy try again, try, please try again, please cry again, what does sorry mean, piggy is sorry, so sorry, full of sorry, Mummy I still feel sorry".

In the last session before the Easter break, she took off her shoes and threw them at me.

I made an interpretation about her anger at me for the break. This seemed to quieten her—that was, until she had to go. She started shouting for mum, punching the seat with her hand: "Buna kick Mum, sorry, sorry, no leave, I am bad, no leave, no leave Baikie, sorry Mum, sorry Baikie, Buna pain in the neck."

Regretfully, this was a much longer break than usual, seven weeks, because I had to take some sick leave. On returning, it was difficult not to feel that there was a huge gulf between us, but Buna was pleased to see me and acknowledged my return. There then followed a number of weeks with very little language: a lot of noises, face pulling, giggling, laughing, with Buna seeming to be feeling very disconnected.

When I was feeling at my most despondent about my work with her, things began to pick up. She became very interested in the noisy boy on one side of us, and the talkative boy on the other. According to their therapists, both boys had an interest in her. It seemed that some life was breathed into us. She began to find language again to describe where she felt she was. Rather than just Baikie, she referred to me as "Aikie, Baikie". She let me know that things were, "Round and round in a circle", "Time, tick, tock, tick, tock, tick, tock". The impact of the time away from each other was felt in the room. As the summer break drew nearer, she shouted loudly at me, "I don't care, go".

When she came back after the summer break, I felt worried and despairing, even. The real spitting had returned. She was slapping and hitting her face, growling and sneering. I wondered what was going on at home. I made enquiries, and what I began to pick up was the workers' growing anxiety. Buna was soon to be 20, and her status would change. She would no longer be within children's services, and she would have to move from her present home. Loss was in the air, and Buna had definitely smelt it.

I began to encounter a much more mocking and cruel side of Buna, and I felt powerless to help her to reach out to the other parts of herself. The terrible spitting continued, and it felt very unbearable when she hit herself. I felt frightened that I had lost her, and then there would be moments of contact between us, and I would see that some part of her battled on against all the odds.

One day she was 35 minutes late for a session. I was worried. They finally arrived. In the session, I explained how much time we had left. She sat very still. She seemed to be reciting some sort of mantra over and over again. It sounded like, "Hurricar". It got louder. She looked at me and said: "Baikie, I said Hurricar". And I realized that while stuck in the traffic and trying to get here, Buna had been saying, "hurry, car".

Soon after this session she began to growl. The growling was unusual, and I talked about the painful feelings deep inside. The behaviours continued, and then, during a particularly difficult session, she looked at me and said, "where we going?" I thought about this with her, where the therapy was going, where she was going, where I was going, and whether we would be going together.

THE CREATIVE USE OF LIMITED LANGUAGE   109

The spitting got worse, and I said that she was spitting everything out: everything seemed to have a bad taste, but that she needed to hold on to it, to swallow. "Sorry", she said. "I am so sorry". She got up, came over to me. I thought she was going to hit me, but she touched my hair and said, "sorry me and you".

The Christmas break got nearer. She started to press her hand against her vagina for a moment or two. Even now I do not want to call it masturbation, but I did call it that to her. I felt braver in the session. I talked about a sexual feeling and this place where she could go and feel nice, away from all my painful talking and thinking.

I talked about the forthcoming holiday break. As she got up to leave, she kicked me. The following session, before I could even speak, she said, " Sorry that I did that, sorry I kick." I was amazed by the syntax. It was hard to keep connected, but during the session she looked at me and said, "doing their best". As she left, she said, "sorry not do it again", the kick still so much in her mind.

Returning after the Christmas break, she was more engaging. I became interested in my own use of words to her, that she had "warmed up", "hotted up", and I wondered where they had come from. I asked her, "how did you get warmed up?" She replied, "me" and touched herself; there was a real sexual air in the room, and she kept referring to the boy next door as "the boy" and saying, "oh boy" to him. Had I become aware of her awakening sexuality without being fully conscious of it in my countertransference?

The following week, Buna did not come. There was no message. I phoned the group home. The answer machine was on. I was concerned, as it was so unlike them. Later in the day, a message came, apologizing. I was struck by what was written on the paper. It read, "it was a cock-up", and I am reminded of my countertransference.

Overview

Buna's psychotherapy continued. There were more losses in front of her, losses that we did not know about but, more dishearteningly, ones we did know about. Loss was in the air, and Buna was an expert when it came to loss. A lack of being understood, a lack of K, impedes learning, but Buna had shown a remarkable ability to make herself understood. We all have many hard lessons to learn, and Buna more than most. What she voiced or spat or even masturbated to me is that knowledge of having learnt how to communicate.

Words can be simple or they can be complex; they can be easily understood or hard to understand; they can be misunderstood. But if words can be listened to and thought about, heard through a mist of rhetoric like the woman at the party or through Buna's use of "pig" and "cow", they can be understood.

I began my professional life as an actor. Buna is the most creative person I have ever worked with. She took what limited resources she had and battled to be understood. With Buna, the impediment of learning was on the other foot: it was I who had to learn. The battle did not bring her happiness or a change in circumstances; it did not make her learning disability go away. She was, however, able to make herself understood, perhaps more than she had ever been. On the other hand, it gave her an even greater awareness of her pain, of her loss and losses to come, though the value of that in itself is debatable. I will end with a quote from Valerie Sinason (1992b):

> Life is full of losses, from the moment of birth we are dispossessed of our first country; the womb. Weaning and displacement by the birth of siblings follows, each new stage in normal development involves loss, starting Junior school means saying goodbye to Infant school. As well as basic losses, we can add the loss of loved ones, country, job, health, underlying all of these is the awareness of our mortality, the eventual loss of our life itself. While some workers in mental handicap have long understood the crucial connection between handicap and loss others have subscribed to the hopeful myth "ignorance is bliss".

Ignorance is not bliss, and neither is knowledge.

Note

1. Makaton is a unique language programme offering a structured, multimodal approach for the teaching of communication, language, and literacy skills. Devised for children and adults with a variety of communication and learning disabilities, Makaton is used extensively throughout the U.K. and has been adapted for use in over 40 other countries.

CHAPTER EIGHT

The question of a third space in psychotherapy with adults with learning disabilities

Pauline Lee and Sadegh Nashat

This chapter is concerned with the concept of dimensions within the therapeutic alliance, and specifically with the problems that arise when the therapeutic relationship is restricted to two dimensions. In psychoanalytic psychotherapy a space needs to exist between the therapist and the patient in order for progress to be made. Within this space, both therapist and patient can reflect on the issues that arise, allowing the therapist to develop insightful interpretations as the therapy progresses. In some situations, however, it becomes difficult or impossible to maintain this necessary distance. As a result, the psychoanalytic encounter may become claustrophobic for both parties, leaving no space for creativity (Symington, 1986). It becomes a situation where there is a lack of symbolic functioning, and primitive psychic mechanisms are brought into play. In theoretical terms, the situation lacks a third dimension, sometimes referred to as the "triangular space" (Britton, 1989)—a dimension within which a variety of desired therapeutic processes could occur. These processes allow for the possibility to make links. This refers to the ability to connect present experiences to past life events and for the patient to realize patterns of repetition, thereby allowing him/her to recover repressed thoughts and feelings. This process involves a transformation of unbearable elements in the patient's experience into meaningful and tolerable states.

As with many aspects of psychoanalytic psychotherapy, the issues for people with and without learning disabilities are basically similar. The life courses of many people with learning disabilities are, however, frequently marked by a variety of factors that place their emotional states in jeopardy. These factors include abandonment, abuse, long-term institutionalization, social stigmatization, inadequate development of coping mechanisms, and impoverished social networks. Indeed, the very term "learning disabled" could be said to freeze the individual in a position of inferiority and dependence on others—a position that is typically viewed as lifelong, no matter how much personal progress is made. Taken together, these risk factors increase the likelihood that the patient will become heavily dependent on the therapist, leading possibly to a two-dimensional alliance. This refers to the potential for the therapist and the patient to be trapped in an unfruitful alliance where there is no capacity for meaning. The case material we present in this chapter demonstrates this phenomenon and the extent to which we were able to deal with it.

"Miss L"

Miss L was a woman in her late twenties who had been placed into care shortly after she was born. She returned to live with her family when she was 3 years old. Her childhood was characterized by repeated abandonment, neglect, deprivation, and sexual abuse. Miss L's father was an alcoholic, and her mother had chronic mental illness for which she was often hospitalized for long periods of time. Miss L had behavioural and learning difficulties at school and was described as having a mild learning disability. She also had a history of drug abuse and sexual promiscuity. Miss L had several attempts at therapy but always was poor in her attendance and/or terminated therapy prematurely. She came into therapy this time as she had requested help with her anger. For the first few months of therapy, Miss L would often dominate the sessions. Not only did she not allow any space to respond or interpret what was happening, it often felt in the room as if there was no space to think. Miss L would talk incessantly, often filling the session with descriptions of graphic sexual and violent acts and paranoid ideas. Initially, she could not recall anything from session to session; it was as though she could not think about the space between sessions. Breaks were also extremely difficult and were perceived as though they did not exist. It was difficult for Miss L to be separate and to allow any space to come between herself and the therapist. It was very hard for Miss L to think that the therapist could be separate from her and have a mind with independent thoughts.

Several people have written about this mode of relating which may help us to understand the underlying processes. Bion's (1962b) theory of thinking has examined what we refer to as the two-dimensional therapeutic relationship. He introduced the concept of two-ness, deriving his ideas from mathematics. His idea is in keeping with the notion central to object relations theories that individual identity is always related to at least one other person. The realization of two-ness is paramount for constituting one's sense of self. For Bion, mother–infant interactions are central to the development of a mind. If for whatever reason the early mother–infant relationship is disturbed, then the development of the infant's capacity to think may be impaired. In psychotherapy such patients have powerful defences that obscure their distinction from their therapist.

Miss L gave a clear example of this. It was difficult for her to experience herself as separate from the therapist; she would either experience the situation as being alone or as being indistinguishable from the therapist.

Jacques Lacan's ideas provide a complementary view on this phenomenon. Lacan (1977) hypothesized a developmental stage called the *"mirror stage"*. Around the age of 18 months, the infant becomes fascinated by its own mirror image and is able to differentiate itself from others, especially its mother. For Lacan, this stage is paramount for the development of the child's ego. Lacan viewed the introduction of the "father's name" into the mother's discourse as being a pivotal event at this stage, because it made the infant aware, in a developing and controlled way, that it is not the sole object of the mother's affection. There is, in fact, a play on words in the French expression "*nom du père*" [name of the father], because it refers not just to the father's name, but also the father's saying "*non*" [no]. Lacan attempts to understand the Oedipus complex from a structuralist point of view, emphasizing the importance of language in the constitution of the individual. For Lacan, the "name of the father", which is the symbolic representation of the father, creates a triangular space.

Britton (1998) explored Bion's ideas further, noting how in some patients a triangular space had failed to develop through a failure of the mother–infant relationship, similarly resulting in an underdeveloped ability to think. He stressed the importance of the failure to establish a place for father in the mother's mind, and mentioned how his findings are close to some Lacanian concepts.

How can Bion's theory of thinking help us further in our exploration of a particular phenomenon encountered in the psychotherapy of a number of adults with learning disabilities?

Bion believed that the first relationship between an infant and its mother creates the possibility for the development of thinking. Through her reverie and receptiveness to the infant's projections, the mother gradually gives meaning to her infant's unprocessed sensations, including those derived from its needs and instinctual drives. Bion called these "beta elements", which are transformed through this process, called alpha function, into "alpha elements": the basis of dreaming and thinking. If this capacity fails, then the infant cannot derive meaning from its experience, or think, and it may then resort to excessive projection in an attempt to rid itself of unbearable anxiety, derived ultimately from its fear of death and destruction. Without relief, this may lead to an escalation, reinforcing its fears and leaving the infant with an experience that Bion called "nameless dread". As a result, the person "feels surrounded not so much by real objects, things-in-themselves, but by bizarre objects that are real only in that they are the residue of thoughts and concepts that have been stripped of their meaning and ejected" (Bion, 1967b). Throughout life the person may repeatedly project their feelings outward—a response that, at best, gives only temporary relief but is also likely to create conflict, hostility, and rejection by others.

Studies of mother–infant observation (Miller, Rustin, Rustin, & Shuttleworth, 1997) lend support to these ideas and give us a good illustration of this process. When mothers show intuitive care and can identify with their babies, they are able to take in their infant's primitive anxieties and through the process of understanding and differentiating real danger from imaginary danger they transform these anxieties into meaningful and tolerable thoughts (alpha elements). In this context Waddell (1998) describes a conflict between "having the desire to know and to understand the truth about one's own experience on the one hand and the aversion to knowing and understanding on the other" that contributes to the development of a thinking mind. When the pain and frustration are too unbearable for the infant, it then becomes impossible for it to acquire a space for understanding and knowing; thereby, it becomes difficult to establish a true sense of self.

This raises the question of the impact on the mother–child relationship when a mother has a baby with a learning disability. Many studies (Atkinson, Scott, Chrisholm, & Blackwell, 1995, Cameron, Snowdon, & Orr, 1992; Faerstein, 1986) have shown the devastating experience mothers can endure when they have an infant with a learning disability. Although some mothers are able to grieve and overcome the loss of their "normal" infant and bond with their baby, there are also many mothers who are unable to do so.

In these cases the mother is unable to identify with her infant and therefore cannot transform the infant's anxieties into thoughts. Additionally, those infants with learning disabilities often have a greater intolerance for frustration. Both these factors contribute to make more likely the experience of "nameless dread" and similar states of mind. This point is illustrated in the case of Miss K, whose discourse is characterized by speech that seems to be empty of meaning.

"Miss K"

Miss K was a 36-year-old woman who had spent most of her life in foster homes and, later, in group homes. There was very little information about her early history, apart from the fact that her mother died when she was a child, after which she was placed in group homes. Miss K has a long history of difficult behaviour and mental health problems, and she has been described as having a moderate learning disability. There have been periods when Miss K has become very disturbed and has shown no interest in her personal self-care of appearance, and she has been very aggressive. Miss K came into therapy as both she and her carers had thought it would be helpful for her to have the space to talk to someone. Her course of therapy lasted only a few months, as it became evident that Miss K was very disturbed and that once-a-week psychotherapy was insufficient to meet her needs.

Miss K would only talk in short or repetitive phrases. She would say things that appeared to have no real meaning: the words and thoughts seemed bizarre. Miss K would say things like, "ghost, ghost, there is a ghost" . . . "Dr Who–who–who" . . . "shit on bread, shit on bread" . . . "measles, I've got measles". Then there would be long periods of silence. The therapist often felt lost, unable to make sense of the words and the meaning. There would often be a feeling of aggression and hostility in the room, a sense that the therapist could not understand Miss K and that she could not understand her anxiety.

It was as though Miss K was left with a "nameless dread", and her terrifying thoughts could not be contained or understood. It also seemed that through the endless repetition of those words, they were empty of meaning: they were meaningless, and therefore they had to be evacuated through a repetitive pattern. Through the repetition, Mrs K wanted to rid herself of her anxiety, but, paradoxically, because of the lack of any meaning, it resulted in increasing her anxiety. This represented for Miss K an endless process that she would reproduce in the transference with the therapist.

Apart from creating potentially lifelong problems for the individual, this added failure of alpha function—both the experience of maternal containment and its internalization—during infancy has profound implications for therapy. As with the rest of life, the patient in therapy has constantly to project unbearable elements, and in doing this creates a "bi-dimensional situation" with the therapist. In this situation, there is no space for the "other" that would create the possibility of an interpretation giving relief and helping the patient's progress towards thinking. Containment of these feelings is crucial if the situation is to change. Without it the patient is imprisoned in repetitive patterns, and free associations are impossible. If, however, the therapist can contain the patient's anxieties and symbolize them, this allows the gradual development of the patient's capacity to recognize his/her self and then to process her/his own emotional experiences. Achieving this shift, which allows thinking, can be very challenging, especially for people with learning disabilities, with their fragile sense of identity. This can be illustrated in the case of Miss L:

"Miss L"

Miss L's experience of a mother–infant relationship was damaged from the beginning. Her mother featured rarely in her life, and when she did, it created a very confusing and terrifying image for Miss L as, in addition to having a chronic mental illness, her mother also had problems with gender identity. Miss L found this very disturbing and held on to personal items belonging to her mother to try to preserve the feminine aspects of her identity.

However, the lack of adequate development of the mother–infant relationship for Miss L meant that she was not able to develop a sense of "thirdness" between her mother and herself. This lack of development also contributed to Miss L's confusion about her own identity. Moreover, she lacked the experience of having a mother who could process her anxieties. Therefore, the therapeutic encounter was experienced as painful, because it invited Miss L to acknowledge that a fundamental process did not take place between herself and her mother.

At the beginning of therapy Miss L spent most of the sessions talking about her boyfriend and what they would get up to together. Miss L would often exclude the therapist from making comments or interpretations by not allowing any space to talk, or to quickly retort that she had no right to say anything.

It was as though she could not tolerate the therapist making a comment about the two of them, as that would introduce another person. Miss L could only relate on a two-dimensional level. The therapist's comments were interpreted as invading that space.

> Miss L talked about R (her boyfriend) coming over and said that they did not have a good evening—she was very angry with him. He wanted to watch a programme on television—a talk show—they were featuring a show with woman with enlarged breasts, with silicon implants. R was admiring them, talking about how beautiful these women were and how big their breasts were. Miss L said she got angry with R and wanted him to change the programme, and he refused. He just sat there watching the programme, admiring the large breasts. Miss L said she got horny and was not into having sex with her man. Then R got horny, and they went to bed. She then said she was not sure about R any more. She remembered that he also liked to watch young children and make sexual comments about them. Miss L went on and on about watching women with big boobs and how watching young children was even worse. It made her feel sick. She kept on using the words "watching" and "feeling sick".

The therapist seemed to be in the same position as Miss L when R was talking to her. Miss L appeared to ignore the interpretation and kept on going on about R, the breast programme, and the young children. The therapist tried again to make an interpretation, that she was like R. Miss L stopped and said, "No, No, you're wrong."

Often Miss L found the experience of being understood as too painful and would defend herself by regressing to a more perverse and primitive state of mind.

Gradually, over time, by finding small spaces within the session to think and interpret, Miss L began to slow down and think more. Interestingly, there was less time spent in the session talking about her boyfriend and more time thinking about herself and the despair she felt about not being able to find a "good-enough partner" and about her life.

"I know I need to come here to talk to someone. It's like talking to a friend; well, it's better than that, because you are trained to listen and talk, aren't you. Talking to friends is different, sometimes you tell them your problems, and they say, yeah, yeah, or sometimes they say something really crazy. You are a therapist who listens and talks back to me. I used to have a therapist who listened and never said anything to me. What good is that? I know you can't tell me to do things or fix my problems or my life, but it helps talking to you, you talk back to me." At this point, the therapist realized that, like many times before, Miss L had talked for a long time, and the therapist often felt blocked by the outpouring of talk coming from her. Miss L said, "You make me think about things afterwards and it helps. It is painful, but it helps."

"You're like a friend, but better." The therapist wondered about her thoughts around being friends and what it would be like. Miss L replied, "I have, you know; I have even thought what it would be like if you and me went to a nightclub together. I said that to the staff, can you imagine me and my therapist going to a nightclub together?" She laughed. The therapist said, "It seems that you are feeling that you do need me, and that we have a close relationship, and it would be nice to think of us as friends. But the reality is that I am your therapist who only sees you at certain times, and that is painful for you to think about, because you wish you could have more."

Miss L uttered "hmm", and there was a long silence. Miss L then said, "I know we couldn't go out. But you do help me. Everyone should see a therapist. I know when I was on drugs my counsellor helped me out a lot. She helped me put my life back together again. She got me to see why I took drugs and why I needed a fix. Now I don't do drugs at all." The therapist said to Miss L that perhaps she saw coming here to see her like taking a drug. She looked at the therapist and laughed and said, "Yeah, you're right. You are like a drug. You're like magic, you are. I always feel better after I leave here." The therapist said it also feels like an addictive relationship that could flip any moment and how this position of being perceived as a good therapist is fragile.

It seemed that Miss L was more able to think about her own identity and her relationships because the therapeutic encounter was not experienced as claustrophobic: rather, it had a tri-dimensional space, allowing creativity and integration of new psychic experiences. Even though her therapy was gradually beginning to work through providing this experience, progress was nevertheless fragile.

Conclusions

In this chapter we have explored one of the important challenges faced by psychotherapists working with individuals with learning disabilities. Alongside their fragile sense of identity, people with learning disabilities have a tendency to form a two-dimensional alliance, which can make it difficult for their psychotherapist to think, create meaning, and understand their patients' experience. We suspect that this has its origin in an added failure, in infancy, of maternal containment, through alpha function, and its further internalization by the infant. It may be that the problems that mothers have in emphatic identification with their learning-disabled children are very important in this process. An added factor, worth further exploration, is the impact on the mother's internal relationship with the father of their having a learning-disabled child. This may lead to a restriction in development of a psychic third dimension.

Unlike in the general population, there is a lack of research and clinical literature upon which psychotherapist can draw. Adults with learning disabilities present many unique challenges in psychotherapy, some of which we have sought to highlight in this chapter. In order to make advances in this area, it will be necessary to complement psychotherapeutic enquiry with well-targeted research studies. Information from such studies could enormously benefit the development of this field, both theoretically and clinically.

CHAPTER NINE

When there is too much to take in: some factors that restrict the capacity to think

Elisa Reyes-Simpson

In this chapter I consider some of the internal and external factors that inhibit and restrict the development of a thinking mind that is able to apprehend internal and external reality. I focus primarily on intellectual restrictions, which seem to arise not as a direct result of organic damage, but due to emotional deficits. The impetus to explore this area came from the clinically painful experience of the disturbance caused to some learning-disabled patients by the process of individual psychotherapy and the potential of close contact with someone wishing to understand them. What became apparent to me in the clinical setting was that the experience of being understood, and through that gaining some understanding themselves, proved too much for some patients.

I first outline briefly some of the psychoanalytical concepts that have informed my thinking.

From the beginning, the baby develops in the context of another. Melanie Klein (1935) has vividly described the infant's exist-

---

This chapter is based on a paper written by myself and Isabel Hernandez-Halton for presentation at a conference in 2000.

ence as characterized by the most primitive anxieties: fear of death, fear of its own desires of love and hate, and uncertainty of survival itself. Development is largely shaped by the infant's experience of these feelings and its ability to process them. This capacity to process feelings is determined by the infant's experience of being known through the mind of another—usually the mother. W. R. Bion's concept of container/contained (1962a) is of much value in formulating an understanding of the development of a thinking mind. He argued that early emotional experience is decisive in terms of the development of a capacity to think. Bion believed that the first form of thinking occurs in the process of striving to know the psychic nature of one's object and oneself. Bion explains that the way in which a mother can allow in and be in contact with her baby's state of mind and is then able to support and respond to her baby allows the baby to grow psychologically. The baby gains the experience of being known through another and attains a meaningful sense of himself and his experience. Implicit in Bion's model of containment is the mother's capacity to be in contact with her own emotional reality. The mother's mind acts as an active container for her infant. The absence of a mother's emotional availability can be experienced by the infant as overwhelmingly threatening to survival itself; Bion described this experience as "nameless dread".

The psychic qualities of the mother's mind and child's mind impact upon one another, and this gives rise to the emotional experience central to the development of thinking. For Bion the knowledge of the psychological precedes knowledge of the physical world: according to him, thinking is not an abstract mental process but the results of a relationship, a human link.

If we see the baby's development as occurring in the context of a relationship with another, development is then greatly determined by mechanisms of projection and introjection. In the early stages of development the primary mode of communication is through projection. The baby has to communicate to the mother all his needs—be they physiological or emotional—non-verbally, and the mother needs to be open to receive these projections or communications and to be able to identify and feel within herself her infant's communications. She has to psychologically and emotionally process this information if she is to be able to respond to her infant and give meaning to his experiences. How does a mother know from a baby's cry if he needs holding or feeding? If he is angry or frightened?

Introjection in this context represents what the baby takes in from the mother following his projections. Through this process a sense of meaning is created between them. The baby's experience of himself and the world is often fragmented, but through his relationship with the mother the baby can develop a sense of integration; the baby develops a sense of himself through being known in the mind of another. Ideally, the mother returns the projections from the baby in a bearable, meaningful form, though there is always a degree of partial failure in this process. However, there are situations where there are factors that impede the creation of meaning. For example, a mother might find it very difficult to tolerate in herself states of conflict and hostility, and this will undermine her capacity to respond to these feelings emanating from her infant; the baby, repeatedly confronted with the fact that its experience is unbearable and intolerable to the mother, will experience parts of itself as a threat and as "unknowable": a disavowal of a part of itself, as if its object fails to introject or miscarries what is perceived or understood about it. I think the baby then introjects this particular experience about itself. What is introjected is an internal structure that is unable to fully apprehend and know. The introjection of such a structure has a determining role in the individual's relationship to knowledge.

Returning to the specific area of learning disability, the questions arise as to how the presence of actual damage affects the container—usually the mother—and how the mother's capacity to tolerate deficit and damage impinges on her ability to mourn the loss of a healthy child and to get on with the normal process of getting to know her baby. Exploring these questions may enable us to isolate factors, which may support parents in facing a very painful situation.

How a mother engages with her baby's real potential is a question that is also applicable to the therapist/patient relationship. As therapists, we have to face the limits of what we can achieve and the limitations of our patient's potential; however, at the same time we hold on to the hope that our patients will develop.

What is often magnified in the contact between a person with learning disabilities and the therapist is difference. Confronting difference may evoke in the patient feelings of envy, and in the therapist feelings of guilt. However, the discomfort of this situation needs to be faced in order for development to take place. Facing difference in most cases means having to tolerate a significant gap in the realistic expectations that the therapist and patient may have of each other.

I think the capacity to apprehend difference, both by the learning-disabled child and by those around him, is a crucial factor in being able to develop the potential for growth, both emotional and intellectual. Parents and professionals alike often feel the need to shield the child or adult from their perceptions of difference, fearing that with a look they will betray a sense of disappointment, resentment, or even revulsion. An example of this is a drive for "normalization" that often rides rough-shod over the child's or adult's actual needs. What cannot be apprehended is the reality of damage. A parent may unconsciously feel unable to make room internally for the child's handicap but may also find it extremely challenging to make space for his/her own sense of damage and guilt in having produced a damaged child. There is, then, a reality for both the child and the parent, which is psychologically "miscarried".

"Mr A"

Mr A, a man in his forties, vividly conveyed this experience to me. He came to me for an assessment for psychotherapy. He explained that he was the middle child from an immigrant family with very high expectations. He had tried desperately to fit in with his parents' expectation that he would "catch up" with his siblings. Throughout his life, he had felt totally overlooked. From what he told me, it was clear that he was seriously developmentally delayed early on, but his parents reassured themselves that he would grow out of his difficulties, and therefore the patient received no specialist help. I was struck by the fact that it sounded as if the professionals around this family also felt that the reality of the patient's handicap was too much for the family to bear, and no attempts were made to offer help. Mr A was keen for me to understand his pain at feeling that his parents could not take in the reality of his existence: he felt that his very being was cruelly disavowed. Mr A came wanting help with his sense of enormous rage and impotence with regard to this. He complained bitterly that he wished his parents had been able to see that there was something wrong with him. He expressed his despair and a sense of feeling absolutely stuck, he feared that no one would be able psychologically to "take him in". In the assessment he conveyed to me a belief that he is perpetually surrounded by damaged figures, too weak to understand him. It is likely that Mr A's parents may have felt externally and internally bereft of the resources necessary to manage the sad task of facing their son's limitations, their painful feelings of disappointment or even shame. In the to-and-fro of everyday contact, the presence of damage is constantly being projected and introjected. In this scenario this process was, I think, severely distorted and driven by a need to obviate the truth. It is important to stress that the motivation and force to deny reality are usually unconscious.

With Mr A I have described some of the concrete ways in which the need to deny manifests itself and how this undermines the possibility of development. I would now like to describe a more subtle process, which may occur in the face of unpalatable truths. In a situation where the need for denial is of the utmost importance, there can often be a pull to identify with the "denying object". This identification may have a protective function, as if needing to protect one's object from a different perception. As a consequence of the denial of disability, it is then very difficult to identify with the need for help.

"Mr B"

Mr B was referred for treatment with a view that he needed help in getting on with his life. Mr B had a mild learning disability and appeared to have considerable skills. Potentially there were many possibilities for study and work open to him.

However, he had found it impossible to have realistic aims and make plans. Mr B came across as omnipotent and painfully out of touch with his situation. He had in fact suffered from a manic psychotic breakdown, which had required hospitalization. He had initially presented in a hyper-manic state, which was then followed by a period of feeling very persecuted, fearing for his life and believing that he was being robbed of his finances. Care staff supporting Mr B were at their wits' end in their efforts to help him to take appropriate steps, especially as he quickly substituted all realistic plans with plans for "executive jobs with grand lifestyles". Everyone around Mr B felt frustrated that nothing could come to fruition. Mr B himself was also very stuck.

After establishing that Mr B's mental state was under adequate psychiatric management, I began to see him for once-weekly psychotherapy. Mr B found it difficult to engage in this work, often retreating into fantastical thoughts whenever his painful reality came into view. As work progressed and he began to be able to be more in contact with the reality of his situation, Mr B became very preoccupied by thoughts that his mother was furious with me, and he warned me that she would be coming to "bash my head". He explained that his mother was not happy with the content of our sessions; he also conveyed that she felt threatened by our work. Mr B was emphatic that he and I were in danger. It may have been the case that in reality the patient's mother disliked Mr B's contact with me; however, in my contact with him I felt that the mother Mr B was referring to was an aspect of himself in projective identification with a scotomizing figure. The work with me disrupted an internal situation that requires the denial of reality and leads to a violent need to murder the eyes that see. Mr B conveyed to me that the "mother" aspect to which he referred also felt persecuted by his limitations and sense of damage.

As I mentioned earlier, in the therapeutic relationship there is often a pull to re-enact these internal situations. We may, in fact, be involved in a re-enactment when we find ourselves feeling sleepy when with a patient, as if literally switching off from contact with him, or when we feel full of despair and feel the only course of action is to terminate the treatment. These states of mind may portray an experience of an internal situation in the patient.

"Bella"

Some of the issues raised above are illustrated in greater detail in my work with a young woman referred to our service for psychoanalytic psychotherapy. I shall refer to her as Bella. Bella has been engaged in once-weekly psychotherapy for just over a year. She is in her early twenties and has a mild learning disability, the cause of which is not known.

Bella was referred by her local psychiatrist, who described her as having great difficulties in sustaining relationships and applying herself in general. She had also in the last months put herself at great risk by repeatedly placing herself in vulnerable situations. She was described as suffering from extreme mood swings. She appeared also to switch off or literally to run away in the face of distress.

Bella comes from a very deprived background. Her teenage mother abandoned her shortly after her birth. She was then placed in the care of relatives and was moved by social services at the age of 10, following an accident when Bella was badly scarred. Until her twenties, she moved to different placements. These broke down, as the carers felt unable to look after her. She often would run way. Bella is now settled with a couple who have informally "adopted" her, and she is anxious to hang on to this placement.

On meeting Bella, she presented as a "chirpy" young woman, pleased to attend and eager to please. She commented on how lovely the building and my room was, and how nice I seemed. She readily expressed her wish to talk to me. At the same time she conveyed a sense of great persecution, with a concern that anything good she has, including the offer of treatment, is precariously held. She responded to my interpreting this during our first meeting by vividly describing how she had been accused of stealing a bicycle. She said this bicycle was in fact her own and that she very much liked it. She told me that two close relatives kept on appearing in a frightening way, out of the dark of night, coming to get her and coming to take the bicycle away. At this point her chirpy façade disappeared, and she became upset. However, the sense of turmoil was short-lived and the defensive façade was soon in place again.

In my first contact with Bella she engendered in me a great deal of confusion. It was difficult to obtain from her a sense of her history and of significant people in her life. The word "mum" was interchangeable and used to refer to various female figures. I used my own sense of confusion to express to Bella that she wanted me to understand what a puzzle there is in her head about her life. She readily agreed and told me that she did not know who her father is, but then with great anxiety and in hushed tones, as if in danger, she said that she did not want to know. From this difficult moment she moved on to describe items of clothing she had just bought. Her affect was again chirpy, yet flattened. This turning to concrete descriptions of her shopping became a regular feature of the work whenever anything distressing surfaced.

From my initial assessment meeting I was struck by two salient features. One was Bella's great attempt to maintain herself and her objects on a friendly and happy note with a sense of having a very precarious hold on anything good. Secondly, her great sense of confusion seemed primarily to offer comfort—as if in order to hang on to something good, she needed to maintain herself in a rather confused position.

Through this process Bella appears in practical terms to have rendered herself unable to engage fully in life and to apprehend fully her reality. She survives an anxious existence while at the same time needing to turn a blind eye to her real situation. As a consequence of this she exposes herself to concrete danger, as described in her referral.

From the assessment I wondered: What is the confusion defending against? What does she have to be switched off from? And why is her sense of a good object so precariously held and so fiercely fought for?

I have begun to unravel some of these questions through my understanding of Bella's experience of me and of the treatment as a whole.

Bella's contact with me is fraught with her constant preoccupation with my state, a concern as to whether I am all right. She has shown a great determination to get on with me on a rather flat and concrete basis. Her friendly good mood has a desperate quality to it. There is a pressure to maintain this façade, as if the alternative would be a catastrophe for us both.

I have often interpreted this to her: her fear that her disturbing feelings would be too much not only for her but also for me, as if there is a reality we cannot face. I think Bella needs to keep me "nice" in her mind at the expense of depth. An example of this occurred early on in the work, when Bella came up close to me. She asked me to look at her pretty necklace, inviting me to ignore the horrific and painful background of her scarred neck. It was as if she was inviting me to look at her but to disregard any damage, to focus on something nice.

I took Bella's need for "niceness" at the expense of depth as a communication of an early object relation. Here I use the concept of object relations to describe an internal representation of significant figures and relationships from the past with their concomitant emotional associations. Bella communicated to me the existence of an internal structure that prevents her from moving to a depth of understanding and knowledge. Internally she has an experience of being with an object that cannot know her and also tolerate knowing something of it's own experience. Depth would mean having to confront painful unbearable truths. If I return to Melanie Klein (1935), she describes early infantile experience as characterized by the dominance of primitive anxieties. The baby needs an object to make overwhelming frightening experience bearable and knowable. It seems likely that for Bella this relationship to an object is lacking or deficient. Anxiety has not been mitigated by the maternal function of containment. The failure, and at that moment the absence of a containing object, becomes the presence of persecution and dread.

Melanie Klein has explained that the infant needs initially to protect his good object by using one of the most primitive defence mechanisms, namely splitting, needing to keep the good and the bad strictly separate. Thus the mother who nourishes is not perceived as also being the mother who frustrates. The infant makes an important developmental stride when he is able to integrate the two and can be said to have been able to introject a whole object. This is achieved if the mother can make hate, fear, and aggression knowable. If the "bad" is made to be more bearable, then the good object is also felt to be more sustainable. However, with Bella, I think we have a situation where she experiences the knowledge of the "bad" as the catastrophic loss of the "good". She needs to keep at bay any depth for fear that unimaginable persecution and destruction would ensue and all goodness would be lost. In terms of primitive anxieties, this would also be experienced as a threat to survival itself.

I think Bella very much experienced what I have described in relation to me in the transference. She constantly feared that I would be lost to her as a good object if her negative feelings emerged. This clearly manifested in her difficulty in remaining with me in the sessions. I think she needed to leave prematurely in order to protect us both. The work itself felt to her to be a threat to her precariously held good objects.

Bella's self-exposure to external dangerous situations in cut-off states I think also manifests her functioning by splitting. She disavows any knowledge of aggression and hatred. I believe that her self-exposure to danger may also have been an enactment of a state of mind, a relationship with an internal object that wishes her dead.

The cost to Bella of keeping herself in a state of confusion and superficiality is great in terms of the limitations it places on her life and development. But for Bella the cost of facing her internal and external reality feels much greater. She fears being exposed to a psychological catastrophe.

Bella has struggled to continue to attend her sessions. There have been some shifts in her capacity to integrate her experience. On one occasion following a period when her treatment with me was in great danger of being discontinued because of her difficulties in attending, she said, "I have had horrible ideas about you, I have said bad things. I'm sorry. I like it here." I interpreted her relief at my persevering with her in the face of her bad thoughts. In response to his, she began to describe how ugly and sore she felt.

Conclusion

It is important to emphasize that the processes I have described are central to all of our development. However, the task for the mother with a learning-disabled infant may be greatly hampered by the unpalatable truths that have to be faced. The internal resources needed to comprehend, digest, and mourn the reality are taxed to the fullest. The patients I have mentioned portray some of the difficulties faced in the process of development, which potentially lead to further intellectual and emotional deficits over and above their initial disability. It is important to bear in mind that the patients discussed cannot be considered as representative of the whole population of people with learning disabilities, most of whom lead fulfilled and meaningful lives. However, I think these particular examples highlight some of the emotional hurdles that need to be negotiated. In the cases I have described, the emotional difficulties were compounded by concomitant social and economic deprivation.

The re-enactments of internal situations that I have described in the therapeutic setting also occur in our everyday life. However, in the psychoanalytic setting we have the opportunity to explore and to understand what the re-enactment represents and communicates. This work requires the therapist to be receptive to the primitive feelings evoked in him or herself—for example, the wish to be rid of the patient, feeling invaded or overwhelmed, deadened or cut off, and to create the mental space to think about a communication that to the patient is felt to be unthinkable. This work also requires us to face our limitations and to manage despair when there is no hope of change. This situation is not unlike that of a mother with a disabled infant. The capacity to process unpalatable truths facilitates emotional and intellectual development and enables us to hold on to realistic hopes.

CHAPTER TEN

An exploration of severe learning disability in adults and the study of early interaction

Lydia Hartland-Rowe

This chapter is about difficulties in acquiring and holding on to knowledge and about the role of early interaction in the development of a capacity to learn, examined by drawing on both psychoanalytic and child development sources.

Working with adults with severe learning disabilities prompted my interest in this exploration. The role of early interaction in the development of their profound difficulties in thinking and learning is a matter of distant speculation. The individuals I describe had their own unique experience of learning not to learn, and for each one a significant part of the process had taken place years ago and is now, sadly, unknowable. What I do have available, however, from my work as a music therapist and residential social worker, is clinical and observational material that illustrates the difficulties for my adult clients in thinking and "knowing". With the use of this material I identify and illustrate certain powerful themes in learning disability that recur and are significant and I speculate about links with early experience.

I start with a series of vignettes: descriptions of contact with learning-disabled adults in which various themes emerge. Although they are descriptions of real events, these vignettes do not always come from isolated clinical encounters: some of the examples described occurred not just once but again and again, with little variation. These repeated, rather barren interactions seemed to be so much a part of life that they could go unobserved. It became acceptable and even expected that human interactions—normally a place where at least a degree of uncertainty is a central quality—could become ritualized and deadened through repetition. An effort to convey this is one reason for choosing to use vignettes, rather than examples of more detailed material. An additional argument for this model is that the vignettes highlight the difficulties I am describing as they occur in a more-or-less neutral setting.

The vignettes are grouped according to themes concerned with difficulties in gaining or holding on to certain kinds of knowledge and raising some questions about learning and relationships. With this material in hand, I then turn to child development and psychoanalytic sources to discuss the impact of the earliest relationships on learning ability.

Observational material: work vignettes

The setting in which I worked was a therapeutic home for learning-disabled adults with emotional and behavioural difficulties. Some of the residents had difficulties with a clear organic root, such as Down's syndrome, but others had no clearly identified organic disorder. Some had experienced serious trauma, in the shape of appalling experiences in institutions, of bereavement, or of abuse. Others had escaped these traumas and had lived at home until young adulthood, in highly dependent relationships with their parents.

The structure of the setting meant that there was a high staff–client ratio, with an emphasis on planned, focussed, and gently supported activity. There was an ethos of space and choice and some recognition of the need for individuals to develop at their own pace. It was possible, in this essentially facilitating environment, to notice patterns of behaviour and functioning that seemed to be shared among members of the group. A battle seemed to take place within these adults—a battle for and against knowledge about themselves and the world they inhabited. The levels of what could be known at any given time seemed to vary enormously from individual to individual and even within the same individual at different times.

My observations highlight three areas of difficulty: in making physical use of the world, in doing things alone, and, in apparent contradiction, in doing things with someone else (not disabled) present—that is, in using help without becoming completely passive. Underlying all of this was also a quality of fluidity—a marked and seemingly inexplicable fluctuation between capacity and incapacity.

Knowledge of the body

One notable feature of physical difficulties experienced by residents of the hostel was that these were rarely just physical restrictions. Although some of the residents were physically disabled, their difficulty in approaching tasks and everyday activities was rarely simply a question of "can't reach that" or "don't bend that way". Instead, the problems of physical action seemed more to do with motivation and often, it seemed, with the difficulty in coping with the presence or absence of another, more capable mind or body. This affected even simple tasks.

Vignette 1: "Will"

Soon after I started to work at the home, I was helping Will to dress. He sat on his bed and lifted up each article of clothing, holding it in front of him as though it were a foreign object, completely mysterious. I ended up giving him a lot of assistance. As we got to know each other and I became more aware of his capacities, his approach to these puzzling objects became more elaborate: he would put trousers on over his arms, shirts back to front. As these efforts became increasingly intricate, I felt that physically he was capable of dressing and gradually gave him less and less assistance. He would appear with not just one jumper on but five, one on top of the other—an extremely difficult operation and much more complicated than just one.

Vignette 2: "Suzanne"

Suzanne, a young woman without physical handicap, would be shown each morning painstakingly how to put on pants, tops, socks, and would manage with only a token bit of physical assistance. If she was left to herself she would sit, passive, waiting, it seemed, for someone who would think about, and do, the act of dressing.

For Will and Suzanne, the problem was not a lack of understanding of the process of getting dressed, or a physical incapacity. It seemed to be something to do with volition—ultimately, with thought. There seemed to be a real disparity between what was physically possible and what seemed to be emotionally feasible.

Vignette 3: "Ken"

Ken, who came to the music therapy session regularly in his wheelchair, could sometimes open the door himself, manoeuvre himself into the room, and shut the door. At the ends of sessions, however, when it came time to leave, he had great difficult in performing the same physical actions, becoming increasingly passive and clumsy.

Here, the variation in capacity suggests that an emotional component to an experience could influence the ability to function well physically. On the way towards something that was a good experience for Ken—his music therapy session—he seemed to use his mind and body well: on departing, he was less present for himself.

These experiences of physical difficulty, which were repeated many times and in different contexts and relationships, seem to show that there is some factor influencing the capacity to hold on to and use physical knowledge. They seem, too, to show that this concerns a relationship, and that it is highly variable. The idea that knowledge of the body—in some ways the most fundamental area of knowledge—could be so dramatically influenced in the context of a relationship suggests a fundamental link between emotional experience and physical learning.

Knowledge and being alone

The difficulty of being and doing alone appeared to be a central one in this setting. It was very rare for anyone to do anything alone. For some people, time alone was spent in passive engagements, like watching television. For others, even this was not possible.

Vignette 4: "Ken"

Having bought a Walkman and chosen the tape for it, Ken would sit for hours, fiddling with the buttons and poking at the innards of the Walkman, not listening to the music but being engaged in a concrete and yet mindless way with the machine itself.

Vignette 5: "Peggy"

Peggy was taught at her day centre to make a woollen doll—not quite knitting, but an attractive piece of craftwork and well within her capabilities. She came home eager to keep this work going but could not do it or want to do it unless someone was with her.

Vignette 6: "Will"

The only thing Will expressed any wish to do was to be driven around in the car. If a walk was proposed at the end of the drive, he could sometimes get involved and interested, but he seemed to need the thought to come from someone else. His idea seemed to be about being a passenger, not a traveller in his own right.

This need for someone else not only to provide the initial spur to become engaged in any activity but then to sustain the interest in it was an absolute and constant quality of the experience I had with this group of people. It felt as though without the initiative of members of staff, nothing could happen. People leafed through catalogues, although there were books for those who could read or used to be able to do so, and other visual materials were available for those who couldn't. Endless soap operas were watched with apparent indifference, although Suzanne, who could not remember how to dress each morning, could describe, in great detail, complicated family relationships, marriages, pregnancies, quarrels, and love affairs from any number of soaps. It was extremely rare for any of the residents to prepare themselves even a snack. This may have been partly a painful echo from years of institutional life when access to food was restricted, but it felt more as though it was impossible for people to have an idea of something for which one could have an appetite, and then go through the process of active anticipation and preparation. In nearly all situations, however, if a member of staff took the lead, was active and aware, then there could be a kind of engagement with active living. It seemed that, at root, what was most wanted was, simply and primarily, contact. It was a certain kind of contact, however: rarely the contact of two collaborators, or even of teacher and pupil. Rather, the contact that was perpetually sought was of a kind of being glued together, being the same.

Knowledge and being separate

I have drawn a distinction between "being and doing alone", as described in the examples above, and "being separate", as described in this section. It was the area of difficulty of which I was most aware in my work. My observations seemed to tell me that, although desperate for contact in the way that I have described, my clients then found it very difficult to be themselves, to be separate in any positive or life-enhancing way. I think this is evident in the examples of Will and Suzanne dressing in the morning: in the presence of a potentially helpful other they could, it seemed, only be passive, or active in a perverse way.

I found this most apparent in the context of music therapy work, where the channel of communication is usually through joint music-making. Improvising in this way should offer the patient an opportunity to explore a mode of self-expression, heard, supported, and amplified by the therapist. What I found repeatedly was that this kind of joint creativity was not possible. Alone, individual patients seemed to re-create, both musically and in their use of me and of the room, all the difficulties in communication and emotional vitality with which they struggled elsewhere. Joined in musical activity with me, they seemed just to disappear, losing any sense of identity. Instead of being able to hear and support and join with their voice as expressed through the materials, I would invariably find myself with a kind of musical passenger—someone glued to me absolutely, not able to use any of the rich and laden opportunities offered through the use of sound (changes of pitch, rhythm, intensity, even volume). This seemed to be a mindless and empty experience, only useful, I felt, in making it clear just how profound the difficulties were for my patients in simply being themselves.

Vignette 7: "Andy"

Andy would sit at the piano and, for minutes on end, would twiddle two fingers on the keyboard, not looking, not appearing to listen, just twiddling and twiddling. He would do this if left space in which to play alone, but when I attempted to join him and to provide some sort of musical frame for what he was doing, even this tiny, monotonous voice would simply disappear: he would either stop altogether or become terribly excited by what I was doing.

This is a typical example of the difficulty my clients seemed to face in being separate. This experience of there not being room for two creative minds was paralleled elsewhere when it came to knowing things. A fairly typical experience in working with people with learning disabilities is to be asked the same question many times, even in the same interaction. Obviously it is important to be aware of the possibility of some organic contribution to brain functioning that makes short-term memory problematic, but on occasions the move from "stupidity" to knowledge, and even wit, was remarkable.

Vignette 8: "Ken"

We were in the car on our way to a holiday destination. Every time we passed a mileage sign, Ken would ask, "How far is M___ton?" and was told the number of miles (he could not have read the numbers). Immediately after having been told, he would ask again what the sign had said, as if he had no way of holding any of this in mind. These rather deadening encounters somehow lacked the vigour of a child's insistent "Are we there yet?" and felt more as though a spark of interest was immediately crushed by a kind of thudding mindlessness. After many hours of this, however, we passed a small road sign with a picture of falling rocks—very quickly, Ken shouted out, "Mind your head!"

This display of real quick-wittedness, following so closely on the heels of what appeared to be utter empty-headedness, left me curious about what it was about thinking, and knowing, that was so problematic, that left Ken having to "mind his head". It is important, as Valerie Sinason (1992b) points out, to recognize the fluctuations in the mental capacity of any individual, learning disabled or not, but I was often aware of what I felt was a particular difficulty for some of my clients in knowing their own minds in the most basic sense.

Vignette 9: "Ken"

Ken was sitting looking at magazines with Anne, a new, very pretty young social work student who had just started a long work placement in the home. He turned a page, asked, "What's that colour? Is it red?" (he was most particular each morning about what colour T-shirt he would wear; he knew his red, blue, and even mauve from each other). Anne answered patiently that no, it was blue. Minutes later, he asked again what a colour was, was it blue, and again, patiently, she answered that no, it was red. This interaction (extremely painful to witness), went on for some time; the same question asked repeatedly, and answered conscientiously, as if it really was not possible for Ken to hold these simple thoughts in his mind.

I became interested in the idea that difficulties in learning and thinking are something interpersonal, happening in the context of a relationship. What seemed to be happening to Ken's knowledge of colour was happening in the context of his contact with Anne. In the same way, she seemed to be caught up in a dialogue where knowing things and holding on to them felt impossible: she appeared unable to hold on to the idea that Ken could *know* the things she had just told him.

Vignette 10: "Ken"

After several years of music therapy with Ken, we had a session during which he really became engrossed in a group of percussion instruments, checking out the sounds they made, trying things out, exploring in a way that was not just sensual, and was not simply trying to get something mindless and exciting going with me. This was very rare and felt precious. I did not play, I just sat and listened, moved by the experience of being with someone who had a little bit of their own mind and their own creativity. At the same time, this seemed so fragile that I felt I could not safely join in without somehow shattering something.

These experiences seem to suggest that difficulties in learning and thinking take place in the context of relationships, and that this affects (1) the ability to relate physically to the world, (2) the capacity to function alone, and (3) the ability to maintain separateness, whether alone or in the presence of someone else. Having had these experiences with adults, where it seemed clear that difficulties in learning and thinking occurred in a the context of relationships, I found myself increasingly curious about what kinds of early experiences in relationships might influence the course of cognitive development.

I wondered, as a starting point, what effect an organic dysfunction might have on early interactions. Some of the difficulties might present themselves on a physical, although almost microscopic level. What might it feel like, for example, to hold an infant, who, because of cerebral palsy, is either constantly jerky in a way that doesn't feel linked to the mother's physical care in holding him, or floppy and apparently unresponsive to her physical attentiveness? When a baby seems to "respond" in this way (albeit involuntarily), how does his mother's emotional experience of this affect the image she has of herself as a mother, and of the child? Can this image then affect how she actually *does* hold her infant—with more intensity, for example, or with less ease—and how is this then experienced by the infant? Quite apart from this physical spiral of possible misunderstandings, there is also the considerable trauma and loss potentially associated with the birth of a damaged infant for parents and family, of which Sinason (1992b), Hoxter (1986), and Bentovim (1972, 1975) have written extensively.

Contemplating this complicated and painful spiral led me to another question: what might the effect be of trauma suffered by mother on the development of the infant's capacity to learn—trauma in addition to, but perhaps caused by, the trauma of organic damage or later developmental delay? Here the work of Valerie Sinason is invaluable as a way of understanding the defences against the trauma of damage, for both mother and infant, and particularly the concept of secondary handicap, which may be used defensively to protect against the painful knowledge of difference and damage caused by the initial handicap (Sinason, 1986). Both the initial handicap and the defence of secondary handicap are detrimental to learning.

There is, however, another question, one not addressed by considerations of the effect of organic difficulties on the early dyad, nor even by considering the effect of the trauma of handicap on the dyad and on subsequent cognitive development. How is it possible to think about those difficulties in learning (which can end up diagnosable as severe learning disabilities) that do not appear to have an organic root, or to have cause in external trauma? If the interactions that take place between mother and child can and do provide the material for healthy learning and growth, then is it possible that this contact could also set the scene for a devastating inability to learn—either a reluctance to explore or a defence against knowledge?

Theoretical material

Both the work of developmental psychologists, in discussing observations of mother and infant behaviour, and psychoanalytic theories of containment can be helpful in trying to address these questions. As Broucek wrote in 1979, our greater knowledge about infants is "thanks to the efforts of ingenious experimentalists who ... have developed techniques of putting interesting questions to infants and getting interesting answers" (Broucek, 1979). Twenty years later, there are even more interesting questions and answers addressed by researchers such as Trevarthen (1977, 1980), Stern (1977, 1983, 1985), Hobson (1993a, 1993b, 1993c), Murray (1991, 1992), and Muir (1992)—too many to do justice to in this short account. I would like instead to highlight particular instances in which child development research and psychoanalytic theories about infant development seem to be describing similar processes.

First, I would like to point to what Brazelton, Kosalowski, and Main, in their 1974 paper "The Origins of Reciprocity", described as an "interdependency of rhythms". He noticed that what seems to facilitate a smooth and gradual flow of contact between mother and infant rather than a jerky and inconsistent pattern is something that happens *between* the two, an interpersonal event. Here is a resonance with Bion's account of projective identification as the process by which thoughts are made out of experiences and perceptions (Bion, 1962b). This suggests that alongside experiences and perceptions—the things we feel and do with our bodies, like Brazelton's mothers and babies—there is a process that converts sensation into meaning. Having someone present, with a mind, is what helps to give sensation meaning.

Second, I would like to draw attention to Roger Money-Kyrle's paper on cognitive development, in which he describes the infant as being "predisposed to discover the truth", with a fundamental experience of "recognition" when it finds truth (Money-Kyrle, 1968). He suggests that this first link forms a basis for further cognitive activity. This forms a compelling parallel with Braten's concept of a "virtual other", in which the embryo *in utero* has a sense of an "other" with which it is already able to function in a system of interaction (Braten, 1987). After birth, the infant is then in a process of realizing and recognizing this "virtual other", in a process very like Money-Kyrle's search for truth.

Third, I would like to comment on the emphasis in the work of both Brazelton and Tronick's work on the dyad's capacity to adjust to failure (Brazelton, Kosalowski, & Main, 1974; Tronick, 1989). Brazelton suggests that "the smoothness with which these dyads made such adjustments probably contributed a further opportunity for each learning about the other" (Brazelton et al., 1974). A difficulty in negotiating adjustments could limit the extent to which each member of the dyad could learn about the other and, for the infant, limit its capacity for exploration beyond the dyad. There is a link here with Spillius's account of Bion's three models of thinking about projective identification (Spillius, 1988). She highlights the difference between the first two models, one in which an innate preconception meets realization (as in the search for a nipple), and the second in which it meets frustration instead, which prompts thought. The third model, with the emphasis on maternal reverie and the role of alpha function, describes a process whereby meaning is sought and located. Spillius's point is that perhaps it is possible to link these three models, suggesting that "surely it is repeated experiences of alternations between positive and negative realizations that encourage the development of thoughts and thinking". This seems a helpful parallel to the situation Brazelton describes, where mother sometimes responds to her infant in a way that seems to make a smooth link between them, but where they will sometimes "miss", and the dyad needs to adjust. This adjustment is part of the development of the capacity to learn.

The inhibition of learning

I would like now to turn briefly to an account by Haviland of work with a very passive little girl who lacked affect and left her caregivers feeling that she was not intelligent (Haviland, 1976). Her flatness meant that she was increasingly avoided: cared for, but not stimulated. Haviland observes that it was indeed difficult to play with her or care for her, because she never signalled her desires, "nor ... did she reinforce her caretakers for their care". This pattern of mutual disappointment left her increasingly separate from the world around her. Haviland's clinical intervention focused on affect and on emotional communication, with the result, in the mother's words, that this child "learned to be smart" (clever). Haviland's view was that somehow the child, from infancy, had not been able to "trigger" her mother and carers to meet with her in a process of exploration, and that without intervention the child would have ended up categorized as severely retarded.

What are the factors, then, that can influence the development of the capacity to learn? The process of development happens in company: someone else needs to be present. It is dependent on the real world, on the world of sensation for the infant and on the world of circumstance for the mother. It is dependent on the internal world: on mother's internal landscape and how clearly that allows her to see her baby as an individual. It is dependent on the degree to which the infant is helped to know, in a very simple way, who he is and who he is not, without which he may lack the capacity to be curious about the world. It is dependent, too, on the extent to which experience matches up to the nature of whatever innate expectations the infant arrived with, with the kind of "virtual other" present in the infant.

It is possible to see how a depressed mother, a previously or currently traumatized mother, a damaged infant, a too passive or too active infant could become involved in a malign set of interactions that could result, ultimately, in gross inhibition of the capacity to learn. What remains mysterious is the question of degree. Not everybody with a depressed mother, a physical disability, or an experience of early trauma is left with severe difficulties in learning, nor is every infant whose internal version of the world clashes with experience too harshly. How might it be possible to understand this? Clearly it seems likely that the simultaneous presence of a number of factors is likely to make learning more difficult than would the presence of only one or two. It is also possible that it is the constant repeated experience of a particular kind of interaction that determines the severity of any damage sustained, although there are, of course, many children and adults who, though traumatized by abuse from an early age, are not necessarily severely learning disabled.

The process of human development and early interaction in particular is breathtaking in its sheer complexity. When infant and mother come together in the world, there are so many points of contact, and enormous variation as to the qualities of that contact. A constantly growing emotional history evolves with each multi-faceted interaction, so that in each new encounter the dyad has to reckon with not only what actually occurs between them but to allow the internal processing of these many events.

A useful metaphor is that of a chemical reaction, wherein the atoms in each element make contact with each other. What happens next depends on the nature and number of elements involved and on the number of atoms that will be "in collision". Perhaps if a mother and baby have too many points of collision and too few benign connections, then it is not possible for a compound to be formed. Instead, a kind of explosion could take place, breaking up the capacity to relate and the ability to learn. Contact between mother and child needs to have few enough such "collisions" to allow moments of mutative individuality to hold sway.

It seems clear that the state of mother's internal world is a vital part of this process. If she is somehow unable really to know about what her infant is like, then the infant's capacity to know and learn can be severely affected. I wonder if it is possible for a mother to have a kind of damaging knowledge, to see her infant in such a way that what the infant then sees reflected about himself through mother is something unbearable. This could lead the way to a real struggle against knowledge and an incapacity to learn, thus contributing to the development of a handicapped child who really does then present the world with something very painful and traumatic: damage, difference, lost opportunity, a lack of growth.

The feeling one is often left with in working with adults with severe learning disabilities is frustration at being somehow "too late". Whatever the origins of difficulties, intellectual damage occurs in a very real way. Learning has become exceedingly difficult, the secondary handicap being now a real and inhibiting one, rarely surrendered in the face of enormous pain and anxiety. There can be difficulties within service-providing organizations as a whole in recognizing real difference and damage: in an effort to provide respect and human warmth, difference can sometimes be overlooked rather than faced. This can make it harder still to make contact with clients with real truthfulness, perhaps repeating again much earlier experience of carers not being able to bear to know.

Conclusion

It appears that early interactions, with their multiple points of potential contact, can with geometric progression send development along a particular route. Returning to the chemical analogy, if the "collisions" are relatively few and relatively benign, and if the opportunities missed when collisions do occur are not vital ones, then perhaps the precipitate speed of the progress of any damage can be slowed or adjusted. I have in mind Haviland's little girl, only one year old when she was so close to not learning how to learn. Clinical intervention with this child was successful. This suggests that the role of early mother–infant interaction, with its capacity to facilitate self-knowledge and curiosity, is helpfully kept in mind when encountering infants and children who appear passive, delayed, and lacking in cognitive ability.

Interactions with a severely learning-disabled adult may be taking place in the context of a life with a solid and distressing history behind it. These encounters probably lack the potential for any real, vital development with the fast urgent flow of an infant being helped to learn about the world. It may be helpful, however, in thinking about the experience of severely learning-disabled adults (particularly in the absence of organic damage), to remain curious about the quality of early interactions for these adults and their early object relations.

The field of learning disability is largely characterized by an interest in, and emphasis on, behaviour—on what is observable. By focusing on the ways in which psychoanalytic thinking about the internal world of the dyad connects with the work of child development researchers (arch-observers), I have highlighted the scope for joining up what can become unhelpfully separated in the field of learning disability, the internal and external realities of experience.

CHAPTER ELEVEN

The endings of relationships between people with learning disabilities and their keyworkers

Victoria Mattison and Nancy Pistrang

"A keyworker is a friend that you can turn to, and it's a friend who I can talk to when I've got problems, like what I'm talking to you about, about what has happened in my life—you know, because a lot of things have happened. . . . They're helpful, so to that end it makes one feel that they are different to all the others, and it means that I can turn to them when I've got that many problems or whatever."

This was Jim's account of the role of his previous keyworker, Jean. (All names in this chapter are pseudonyms.) "Jim" was a 41-year-old man with learning disabilities and physical impairment. He grew up in a long-stay "mental handicap" hospital until it closed down when he was in his mid-thirties. He then moved to his home in the community. Jim explained to us that he had had lots of keyworkers throughout his life. He seemed to value the opportunity to talk about his past relationships.

This chapter is based on a book by the same authors, *Saying Goodbye: When Keyworker Relationships End*, © 2000, Free Association Books. We thank Free Association Books for allowing us to reproduce parts of the book.

Here's how Jim talked about how he felt after Jean left:

"I felt lost from hereon... hurtful, very hurtful.... It was like saying, 'I may see you in the future, but I've got to go' sort of thing. 'I know we've been friends, but now it's time to sever our friendship.' I felt gutted, you know, I felt really—I mean, heaven only knows where I go from here.... It was hard, because she was one of my special friends, you know. And we got a sort of close relationship going. It was over a course of time that we got to know each other...."

Of course, not all adults with learning disabilities are so articulate, and many may express their feelings indirectly through their behaviour. However, our research suggests that Jim's experience of loss and hurt is very common.

Our main aim in this chapter is to raise awareness of what happens when keyworker relationships end. Such endings may occur in a variety of circumstances: for example, when a staff member is moving on to a new job, going on maternity leave, or not continuing in their role as keyworker because of a change in staff roles within the home. The chapter is based on a research study in which we interviewed 12 residents and 18 staff about their experiences of the ending of keyworker relationships (for details, see Mattison & Pistrang, 2000). We draw extensively on the words of participants themselves, presenting clients' and staff members' parallel accounts of loss and change. We hope that, with a greater understanding of what happens when relationships end, both clients and staff will be better prepared for the process of separation and will find it easier to say goodbye to each other. Ultimately, our aim is to develop ways of thinking with staff and clients about separations and endings. This thinking applies not only to residential care settings, but also to the separations that we may all experience in all kinds of relationships.

Clearly, not all keyworkers are missed: some clients undoubtedly feel a sense of relief when a keyworker with whom they have not got on well leaves. But, for many clients living in residential care settings, the keyworker is one of the most important figures in their life, and the relationship between them may be one of the closest that clients experience. How the keyworker's departure is handled—for example, how the client is told—can have a critical impact not only on the client, but on other residents in the home, the staff, and the new keyworker who is faced with supporting someone who has experienced a significant loss.

We first describe briefly the context in which keyworker relationships exist, followed by an example from our own clinical work of some of the difficulties in separating. We then present material from our research study to describe clients' and staff members' experiences of the keyworking relationship, how these relationships end, and the impact of these endings on clients as well as staff.

Before we begin, it is worth saying a few words on terminology. Services for people with learning disabilities have adopted the terms "clients", "residents", or "service users" to refer to those receiving services: we use the terms "clients" and "residents" interchangeably. "Keyworker" is the term usually used for a member of paid staff (often minimally trained) who has overall responsibility for the care of a particular client. This usually involves working individually with the client, attending reviews, having contact with families, and coordinating day services. We use the terms "staff" and "keyworker" interchangeably to refer to carers in residential settings.

The context of keyworker relationships

A recent national strategic survey has indicated that one third of all adults with learning disabilities live in staffed homes (Wallace, 2000). A high turnover of staff is a typical feature of many of these residential settings (Allen, Pahl, & Quine, 1990), and it results in repeated experiences of separation for residents. Why is there such a high turnover of staff? Any discussion of the relationships between people with learning disabilities and care staff must take note of the wider political and social issues that are inherent in the context of residential care. Providing good-quality care is not just about policies, procedures, or implementing recommendations; it is also about the importance and respect given to people with learning disabilities as a client group and learning-disability carers as a staff group.

Caring is a function that does not hold high status. Care staff in residential units are often poorly paid, they work long, hard hours, and they receive little training, support, or supervision. The majority of the staff are women, and many are from ethnic minority communities: they come from sections of society that are the least empowered. These staff are expected to implement complicated and demanding arrangements for the management, support, and care of clients with complex needs. The poor conditions of work often lead to burnout, withdrawal, and high rates of staff turnover. One could argue that care staff frequently are devalued, like the clients with whom they work: they are attributed little respect and are not viewed as worthy of training. Such poor conditions of work, and other people's attitudes, can affect the self-esteem of the carers themselves, who may internalize a devalued view of their role.

Clients' relationships with care staff may take on particular importance for those with few other close relationships or none at all. Several writers have expressed concern about the paucity of friendships and close relationships experienced by many people with learning disabilities living in the community (e.g., Atkinson, 1989; Chappell, 1994; Firth & Rapley, 1990; Flynn, 1989). A substantial number of adults, whether living with family or in residential establishments, seem to lack close friends altogether. Such restricted social relationships can lead to a deep sense of loneliness, isolation, and exclusion.

It is not surprising that residents may interpret their relationships with staff members as friendships (Firth, 1986). Such relationships may meet their needs for a close emotional attachment in the absence of anyone else in their lives with whom intimate feelings can be exchanged. In some situations there may be a genuine commitment on the part of residents and staff, which lasts beyond the end of the keyworking relationship. However, the nature of these relationships is not always clear to either party, and each may have a different perception of it. This can cause great distress and loss if the worker moves away, or if the client has perceived the relationship as a friendship, but this has not been understood by the staff member (Firth & Rapley, 1990).

THE ENDINGS OF RELATIONSHIPS   153

Case example: "Ruby"

At the time of our study, one of us (VM) was working clinically with a client whom we shall call Ruby. Ruby was a 56-year-old woman with learning disabilities and long-standing mental health problems. She had spent a lifetime in institutional care, with multiple changes of keyworkers, and she now shared her home with two other clients in a staffed house in the community.

Ruby's referral to the learning disability team coincided with a staff member leaving the home after four years. The team's psychiatrist reported a deterioration in Ruby's emotional state and a return of behavioural patterns that were a cause of concern to the staff and other clients in the home. It was agreed with Ruby and the staff at her home that she would come for weekly counselling sessions, and that we would review our work after one year. About nine months after the counselling started, Ruby's keyworker, Helen, left her home unexpectedly and without warning. Ruby gave us permission to tell the following story about Helen's departure. It is told from the psychologist's point of view.

Helen was Ruby's keyworker and confidante, and they had enjoyed a close and constant keyworking relationship for seven years. Helen was a sensitive and thoughtful young woman who seemed warm and respectful towards Ruby. She accompanied Ruby to most of our counselling sessions, supporting her during her journey and sitting in the waiting-room until we finished our sessions. Ruby would often leave the session for a couple of minutes in the middle to check that Helen was still there waiting for her. She would then return to the room, reassured.

On the day of one of the sessions, Helen telephoned to tell me that she was leaving her job and saying goodbye to Ruby the following day. She had not yet told Ruby. She explained that she had felt very unsupported by the manager and the other staff at the home and that she had found the work overwhelming in recent months. Helen agreed to tell Ruby about her departure before our session that afternoon. Later that day, the two women arrived together for the session as usual, and, as we left the waiting-room, Helen mouthed to me, "She took it very well."

At the start of our session Ruby sat for a moment and began to talk about what she had been doing at the day centre. After a short time I said I wondered how she was and what she understood about what was happening at the home. Ruby stood up and left the room abruptly. I followed her to the waiting-room and suggested that perhaps we could talk together with Helen about what was happening. Ruby seemed pleased with that suggestion and promptly led Helen into the room. I suggested that we might use the time we had together as an opportunity for the two women to say goodbye and to think about the work they had done together and the memories they had of their relationship. It felt difficult to know where to begin, until Helen started to talk about the lovely holidays they had shared, the places they had visited, and the activities they had enjoyed at home. We thought for a moment about what Ruby might remember about Helen. After a brief silence, Ruby looked up at Helen and said simply, "that I liked her". Helen began to cry, and Ruby seemed shocked and became quiet. She then said, pleadingly, "Don't cry, Helen." Helen explained that she was crying because she felt sad to leave Ruby and to say goodbye after such a long time.

Ruby and Helen then began to reminisce together about their past experiences of spending time together, and about the people in Ruby's family whom Helen had met. She explained that she wanted to see Ruby in the future, to invite her to her home and spend time together again. After another few minutes Ruby said that she had had enough of talking and that she wanted to go home. The painful feelings were difficult for all of us to tolerate.

Later that day Helen telephoned from the home. She explained that she had known that it was not right to leave Ruby so suddenly and without warning, but that the circumstances in the home had forced her to leave. She had been worried and afraid about telling Ruby. She was very sad and seemed overwhelmed by her feelings of guilt.

The following week Ruby came to her session as usual. She said straight away, "I feel sad today, because it would be mum's anniversary." She had not spoken to Helen during the week. It seemed that her keyworker's departure from the home had put her in touch with her feelings of loss and grief. After a few moments she asked with urgency, "When are you leaving?" Her confidence had been shaken, and everyone seemed transient to her. I became very aware of the relative brevity of our own contact and the fact that we too had a planned ending in the next few months.

Soon after Helen left, Ruby was allocated a new keyworker in the home, who telephoned me to check when our sessions were planned for the following weeks. During our conversation, I said that I wondered how things had been since Helen left. The new keyworker explained that, due to all the paperwork and plans for transfer of care, she had not had much time to spend with Ruby, so it was difficult to know.

This case illustrates some of the difficulties staff and clients may experience in saying goodbye. It also illustrates that beginnings and endings are an integral part of the life cycle of staff and clients in residential care settings. There are many keyworkers who are clearly good at their jobs throughout the time they work in a home. They may be conscientious and sensitive in all aspects of what they do, but they will often avoid the final task of saying goodbye. This avoidance may arise from their lack of awareness of their own importance to clients or, as Helen's response illustrates, their understanding that saying goodbye is critically important to the emotional world of the client, but quite daunting to initiate. Perhaps the staff are often left feeling uncertain about what to do and how to face some of the pain of separation.

The role of the keyworker

Both the clients' and the staff's accounts in our research study indicated that the keyworkers' roles were varied. This is consistent with previous studies of the roles of care staff (Allen, Pahl, & Quine, 1990; Clegg, Standen, & Jones, 1996). In most instances, being a keyworker was not just about providing physical and practical care, but also involved the development of a personal relationship with the client. The intimacy of residential care work was reflected in how clients described staff, likening them to friends, family members, or even partners in some cases. This sense of intimacy and companionship is evident in the following quotes from two residents:

> "Emily was my best friend.... She used to give me things like soap. She was very nice. We used to speak about everything." ["Sally"]
>
> "[We] go out for a drink, go out for a meal, or go up to London somewhere.... I liked his jokes and his company.... I miss his jokes and company and drums." ["Nick"]

Keyworkers, too, often developed strong attachments to residents—attachments that the keyworkers themselves did not always anticipate when they first started working in residential care. Many staff described, sometimes with surprise, a sense of reciprocity and mutual pleasure in their relationships with residents:

> "With me and Monty there was a definite click, just because of musical interests and he loved going to the theatre.... I had a very good relationship with Monty compared to the other clients, but that wasn't because of being a keyworker, that was simply because Monty was a person that I rather liked.... A lot of people saw the disability. I saw the person." [Tom]
>
> "Just sitting—having a drink—watching the world go by—chatting with each other and things like that.... I think there was a respect there—of my space, my feelings—in the same way as I respected him, I suppose." [Sam]

For staff, the residents' high levels of dependency often felt uncomfortable and overwhelming. This was not so much an issue of being relied on for physical or practical needs, but, rather, an issue of emotional dependence. Some staff members were acutely aware of how much they meant to clients on a personal level: the closeness of such relationships frequently resulted in keyworkers feeling "emotionally overloaded". Other keyworkers seemed to minimize or underestimate their importance to clients, perhaps as a way of protecting themselves from the uncomfortable feelings aroused by their clients' dependency. For example, Oliver, one of the first keyworkers we interviewed, told us:

> "Keyworking a client is a piece of work.... I think I've learnt from 'Simon' [a client] that you can get emotionally attached, and it can be detrimental to the keyworking job. But that's being a keyworker—it can be very hands-on.... I think part of the job is not to get too attached."

Oliver's description of keyworking reflected a sense of his own struggle with the concept of intimacy versus professional distance from clients. He was unsure about how emotionally close one should become to clients within the role of keyworker.

Although the keyworker relationship was perceived in a variety of ways, a central theme running through the clients' accounts was their appreciation of the keyworker as someone on whom they could rely and who had a long-term perspective of their needs. There was a fundamental sense of feeling "known" by the keyworker, and the prospect of having to start all over again with a new keyworker therefore sometimes felt overwhelming.

How keyworkers leave

> "It was very sudden—she just went—like that." ["Audrey"]
>
> "I said goodbye, and she was gone." ["Guy"]

Two-thirds of the clients we interviewed described an abrupt ending, with little or no preparation or chance to say goodbye. Many of the clients were able to comment on their recollections of the absence of preparation. What came through in these accounts was a sense of the suddenness of the change, the not knowing, and the accompanying feelings of confusion, bewilderment, and abandonment.

One could argue that the endings described by residents may have appeared more sudden than they actually were because of the residents' particular needs for lengthy preparation and the provision of repeated and clear messages over time (Emerson, 1977).

However, their descriptions of unforeseen and sudden endings are consistent with the accounts of many staff, who reported either not having said goodbye at all to clients, or who described giving only a few days' notice. For example, Barbara told us:

"The day I left [my first job], the people I was working with didn't know that was my last shift, and none of the residents knew that was my last shift. But the understanding was that the care manager was going to tell everybody.... I was like 'I finish at 8.00 tonight, you know.'"

While some staff were able to carefully plan with clients for the ending of their relationship, many, understandably, found it difficult to know how and when to tell the client and expressed a need for support with this:

"I was having quite a dilemma about how long before I was actually leaving that I should be letting people know. I mean there were no guidelines or anything within the organization... it was very much left down to me. I had to create a kind of wind-down for myself." [Lucy]

Both staff and residents often described how the departure of keyworkers had been marked by pleasant rituals or "happy events" in the home, such as parties or meals out. The importance of attempting to create a "happy ending" was expressed by several staff members, such as Maria:

"There's always an event for the person who leaves, whether we go out for a meal or a party or stuff. It has always ended on happy terms. There's never just a goodbye at the end of a shift. There's always a happy ending. I think people rely on having a nice memory and a happy memory."

However, some staff, as well as clients, questioned how far these events could assist with the pain and inevitability of separation. As one client reflected:

"We did have a leaving party, but that was besides the point you know.... Well, I know, it's not a question of shaking the hand and saying goodbye. It's something more emotional than that, I think." ["Jim"]

Goodbye parties clearly have their place, but they can also be a way of masking or easing the more painful aspects of separation. This may present a dilemma for staff who are wanting to do the best for their clients. Organizing parties and ensuring "happy endings" may be motivated by the staff's desire—conscious or unconscious—to protect their clients, as well as themselves, from the emotional pain of separation. Sometimes it can be difficult for staff to disentangle their own needs from those of their clients.

The impact of separation: feelings of clients and staff

All of the residents we interviewed described painful feelings of sadness and loss arising from the departures of keyworkers. Some spontaneously made a link between losing a keyworker and losing a friend or family member through death. As one resident, "Catherine", put it: *"It made me think of my friend dying."*

Catherine was a 33-year-old woman who had lived in residential care since her early twenties. She was visited regularly by her mother, who seemed to be an important constant in Catherine's life. At the beginning of the interview, Catherine found it difficult to think clearly about saying goodbye to particular keyworkers, because she had experienced so many losses of staff:

> "Lots of keyworkers round here.... Lucy, then Anna, then Mary. Anna—she left, and Lucy, she's left ... she went on holiday herself—to Australia.... She was nice.... I didn't know [that she was leaving].... I always talked to her down in this office. I am thinking about her (*smiles*).... Sometimes I cried my eyes out [when she left].... She sends me postcards. I like that—from Australia."

When we asked Catherine whether she still thought about Lucy sometimes, she said:

> "Yes, but I don't cry my eyes out now—I used to. I was thinking to myself, my friend's died, and my father, and my step-

father.... I don't like people leaving. It's serious.... I didn't want her to leave. I can't stand it.... And I miss Anna, too—because I loved Anna.... I always talked to her in the office.... I feel a bit tired when I'm thinking about it.... I get worried. I don't want staff leaving here."

A recurring theme in the residents' accounts was their lack of control over retaining relationships with staff:

"I don't know why they have to leave when I don't want them to—they have to." ["Sally"]

"I'm sad, 'cause Julia will leave—I'm upset. [Audrey shouted out.] I don't know why she has to leave, because I don't want her to. But Julia does—not me, just Julia.... I am sad. I don't want to hurt her, because she's upset—Julia ... makes me feel sad, just sad." ["Audrey"]

"Guy" was one of many clients who described his longing for staff to return: *"I wish her back."* This longing was often expressed with a painful realization that there was nothing one could do to change the situation. It was out of the clients' control, as "Diana" indicated: *"She can't come back—can't make it."*

Several residents showed insight into the limitations of the keyworking role, and an appreciation (or justification) of staff's decisions to leave. For example, the account given by "Bill" movingly reflects his level of understanding of the keyworker's needs. His keyworker, Sue, had left quite suddenly and it had been a shock to Bill. Nevertheless, he was able to offer a sensitive explanation for Sue's decision to move away:

"She wanted to do a job where she didn't have to do shifts—because when she was doing shifts, she was getting very tired, and when you are very tired, I don't think it's a good idea to start driving a car. Because when you are very tired, you can't concentrate...."

Throughout his account, Bill emphasized the need to "make things nice" and enjoy the ending, because of a danger or prohibition against talking about the more painful aspects of saying goodbye.

This sense of the danger of sad feelings was apparent in many of the clients' descriptions. As Guy said very simply, about his keyworker's departure: *My sadness might hurt her.* Another client, "Lilly", suggested that sadness and feelings of fondness were somehow incompatible: *"I don't feel sad because I like her."* Taken to an extreme, this wish to please or protect the staff seems to negate the residents' realizations of their own rights to experience sadness.

What struck us about so many of the clients' accounts was an implicit sense of compliance and an absence of anger. It may have been difficult, emotionally, for clients to think about how staff's personal situations drew them away from their keyworking roles. The clients may have had not only angry feelings about the separations, but also envious feelings when they considered the lives and opportunities of staff, which differed so much from their own. These emotions were not expressed, although they may have contributed to the emotional pain so often experienced by clients. The clients' accounts give a sense that they "can't bite the hand that feeds them": a fear perhaps that if they do get angry, they might not receive any support. As Sinason (1992b) has suggested, people with learning disabilities often present themselves in ways which are inoffensive and easy going, "for fear of offending those they are dependent on" (p. 21).

The intensity of the feelings expressed by clients was mirrored in many of the staff accounts. Gill described her feelings after leaving her client "Margaret", with whom she had worked for four years:

"I mean, you could say it's like a bereavement in a way. For Margaret it was a bereavement, and for myself as well, really. I mean you've lost a good friend, haven't you? . . . You know, when I first saw her at the club afterwards, I was really sort of choked up and wanted to know all about her. Is she going on holiday? Is she doing this? Is she doing that? And you sort of feel, 'Well, I could be organizing that'."

Keyworkers' accounts suggested that they had not anticipated the extent of their own painful feelings and the element of co-dependency that may emerge within the staff–client relationship. For example, Nia expressed surprise at the strength of her feelings after leaving her client, "Scott":

> "I really do miss him [Scott], and I have found that after a horrendous day here, my automatic reaction will be to go there [her previous workplace]. I don't even think to myself that I'll just pop in. I'm just driving, and then suddenly I find I'm on that road."

Some staff were acutely aware of how their departures—or those of previous keyworkers—affected residents. For example, Debbie observed "Kevin"'s reaction after his keyworker had left:

> Kevin became really quiet. It became really noticeable that he was really unhappy. He completely withdrew from what was going on. It was unbelievable. He was unhappy all the time. He wouldn't eat at the dinner table. He would throw his plate on the floor. We couldn't believe it.

However, for other staff, the painful reality of their own importance to clients seemed difficult to tolerate. This appeared to lead to a process of denying or defending against clients' loss and distress and failing to acknowledge clients' less obvious communications of grief. Striking inconsistencies in some of the staff's accounts suggested a process of denial: they talked perceptively about clients' distress at one moment and then disavowed it at the next. For example, Oliver struggled to attribute emotional reactions to his client, "Simon"—despite obvious manifestations of distress:

> "He [Simon] went downhill after that [Oliver's departure]. He was putting on weight just as I left, and his epilepsy got worse. He probably had two bad years after I left . . . his mum connects that with me going. But I mean, it [epilepsy] always gets worse for a while and then you change the medication and it gets better again."

Oliver seemed to find it hard to consider a link between his departure and Simon's worsening symptoms of epilepsy. At one point during our interview, he reflected on the importance of his relationship with Simon (and other clients), yet moments later he seemed to express contradictory feelings:

"I do tend to get emotionally involved with clients, I really do, because I think empathy is one of the best things you can give to a client. . . . Well, Simon's 45 now, say he's been in care for 42 years, he has probably had a new keyworker every two years, so he's probably had 20 keyworkers. . . . I don't know . . . all this empathy and all the rest of it—I don't think clients, really, I don't know how much they miss you."

It was common for staff to minimize the importance of their roles and their personal relationships with clients. They often suggested that their departure did not matter to clients, as long as the clients' basic needs were met. As one staff member put it, "someone else could fill your shoes very easily". And yet these same staff often indicated a sense of their own indispensability: they feared that new staff would not be able to meet the clients' needs. Flipping between these opposite poles of dispensability and indispensability, staff sometimes seemed confused about what their relationships with clients meant.

What makes it hard to say goodbye?

Historically, it has been assumed that people with learning disabilities cannot form close emotional attachments to others and therefore they will not grieve following death or separation (Oswin, 1981, 1991; Yanok & Beifus, 1993). The stories from residents in our study clearly challenge this assumption. As we have already shown, residents often formed close attachments to their keyworkers. It is not surprising, therefore, that the loss of these relationships led to a process of grieving.

However, expressing grief through words will be difficult for many people with learning disabilities. As Harper and Wadsworth's (1993) study of bereavement indicates, clients with limited verbal communication often express their grief through their behaviour—for example, by hitting out or withdrawing. Some of the staff in our study recognized clients' behavioural expressions of distress, both immediately after hearing the news that keyworkers were leaving and in the aftermath of their departures: they observed clients regressing to lower levels of functioning or withdrawing completely from interactions with others. Other staff, however, were unaware of, or puzzled by, behavioural expressions of grief: they seemed to assume that in the absence of obvious expressions of sadness, clients did not grieve.

In view of the painful feelings aroused by endings, it is not surprising that some staff seemed to deny, or minimize, the impact of their departure on clients. Their fluctuations between awareness and denial of the impact of loss seem to reflect how uncomfortable it can be for staff to think about their roles. Rosenberg (1990) suggests that staff working with disabled clients have a natural tendency to avoid thinking about emotionally painful issues related to disability. The reality of the client's long-term dependency is perhaps too painful for everyone concerned and may lead to the care worker's avoidance and denial of the client's feelings of grief. Terry (1997) also points out that it can be difficult for carers to think about the meaning of clients' difficult behaviours because of the "unbearable feelings" underlying such behaviours. He urges staff to think about and understand difficult behaviours as communications, rather than attributing them to organic causes or personality problems.

The organizational systems in which staff work may also contribute to their tendency to minimize their own importance. As Menzies (1970) has proposed, the structure and culture of an organization can protect its members from uncomfortable feelings such as anxiety, guilt, or uncertainty. Such aspects of the organization are referred to as "socially structured defence mechanisms". As in the nursing system observed by Menzies, the nature of residential care systems—for example, the frequent changes of staff rotas and the emphasis on the practical tasks of keyworking—may promote a sense of depersonalization, which protects staff from the painful feelings evoked by their contacts with clients.

Many of the staff we interviewed told us that they had few opportunities to think about and discuss their roles and the process of leaving with more experienced colleagues or managers. It is not surprising, therefore, that they often ended up feeling overwhelmed by their responsibilities and by the feelings that the work aroused. If clients' distress over separations is to be reduced—and if sudden departures and a high turnover of staff are to be prevented—then services must think about supporting and valuing the staff themselves. Clearly, regular supervision, team meetings, and informal opportunities for discussion are crucial. This may seem so obvious that it is hardly worth mentioning, yet we know that, in practice, the needs of staff are often overlooked.

In the course of our research, many staff expressed the need for guidelines on managing endings. The first-hand experiences recounted by the clients and staff in our study could provide a starting point for thinking about ways of planning and preparing for separations. Clearly, there are several key aspects of the ending process that need to be considered: telling the client, recognizing the client's feelings, recognizing one's own (the keyworker's) feelings, and making plans for the client's future care. Services also need to consider some broader issues: the importance of thinking about the nature of the keyworking relationship, expanding clients' social networks, and providing support, supervision, and training for staff. These ideas about how to manage endings are discussed in greater detail by Mattison and Pistrang (2000). In developing any guidelines, it is important to remember that individual staff members work not in isolation, but within complex settings that influence how they interact with their clients. Without support and training, and without continued discussion about what the work is all about, care staff will struggle to carry out the demanding responsibilities of their jobs. Staff teams themselves must be "cared for" in order to enable them to provide the best care possible to their clients.

Conclusions

Saying goodbye—that is, talking with people with learning disabilities about the process of ending and helping them to understand their feelings—is crucial if clients are to develop new relationships in the future. Like clients, care staff also often feel a sense of loss when their relationships end; unless these feelings are recognized, it can be hard to begin working with new clients. The process of grieving can be particularly important for people with learning disabilities, who may be sensitized to loss because of multiple losses in the past. Clients' histories may thus make staff departures particularly painful, leading them to feel wary of forming new emotional attachments. Sensitively planned endings, therefore, are essential in order for clients to continue to be able to trust and become close to others.

Facing the difficult issues of endings can ultimately empower clients. The emotional pain of separation can, of course, never be eliminated, but preparation and support can enable clients to adjust to loss and develop skills for coping with future relationships. Endings can provide an opportunity for keyworkers and clients to think together about what has happened during the course of their work and what is wanted or needed in the future (Fredman & Dalal, 1998). If clients are enabled to take a more active part in the process of saying goodbye, they may feel a greater sense of control over their lives in general.

CHAPTER TWELVE

Ensuring a high-quality service: clinical audit, quality assurance, and outcome research in the Tavistock Clinic Learning Disabilities Service

Nancy Sheppard, Sally Hodges, and Marta Cioeta

Recent developments in clinical quality assurance and governance have particularly dictated that an important part of any service provision is the inclusion of means of monitoring and ensuring high-quality, meaningful and effective services. Since the launch of the Tavistock Clinic Learning Disabilities Service in 1995, we have organized methods to monitor various aspects of the service, including the psychotherapeutic treatments we are providing. This chapter aims to explore some of the methods available in assessing or evaluating our work and to give an overview of the projects we have already undertaken. We will discuss some of the issues that have arisen as a result of our evaluation projects and attempt to relate our dilemmas to wider issues in research with people with learning disabilities and services for people with learning disabilities.

Clinical audit and quality assurance

Clinical audit is the approach whereby one measures the effectiveness of clinical activity by comparison with a pre-set standard. This can be achieved by deciding in advance what standards or criteria for local practice should be, then by monitoring how frequently these criteria are met. Audits are helpful in getting an overview of the effectiveness of local services and in considering service development. Firth-Cozens (1995) provides a good introductory text to audit in mental health services, and Davenhill and Patrick's (1998) book provides examples of more advanced audit techniques.

The Learning Disabilities Service at the Tavistock Centre has undertaken two clinical audit projects over the past five years, and these have given some interesting results and helped us to think about some of the dilemmas of offering a psychodynamic psychotherapy service to people with learning disabilities and their carers.

Attendance audit

As an ongoing measure of service delivery, we decided to audit the numbers of clients not attending appointments (DNA rates) and cancellation rates. DNAs are classified as appointments missed without an explanation given prior to the appointment. These rates were compared to the DNA rates in another department in the Clinic to give a sense of how our service relates to others.

A random sample of 22 open cases was audited. These were selected by taking alternate files from the current caseload of the team. It was considered that a 5% DNA rate was acceptable (i.e. clients missing one out of every 20 appointments).

For each of the 22 cases selected, an attendance report was assessed, noting

1. the total number of appointments offered in each case,
2. the total number of DNA appointments,
3. the total number of appointments cancelled by the client, and
4. the total number of appointments cancelled by the therapist.

Results

In total, 750 appointments had been offered to the 22 individuals whose files had been used for the audit.

DNA rates

Of the 750 appointments offered, 84 had been recorded as DNA—an overall DNA rate of 11.2%. The standard deviation for this sample was high, varying between 0% and 41%. On further analysis of each case, 30% of cases had no recorded DNAs, and only 31% had a rate of over 5%.
This compares to a rate of 35% in the other department.

- *Cancelled by patient rates*

 The total percentage of appointments reported as cancelled by patients was 8.5%; again the standard deviation was high: individual rates varied between 0% and 28%.

- *Cancelled by therapist rates*

 The total percentage of appointments cancelled by therapists was 2.5%; this result was further analysed to reveal that of the therapists offering therapy, 55% had never cancelled an appointment and a further 32% had cancelled only one appointment.

Referrers' survey

This survey was considered both important and timely, considering the unique service offered by the Tavistock Learning Disabilities Service and the growing interest in psychoanalytic and psychodynamic psychotherapy for learning-disabled people in the United Kingdom (Nagel & Leiper, 1999).

The Tavistock service commissioned the survey for two reasons:

1. in order to investigate the effectiveness and quality of the referral process;
2. to elicit the referrers' views of the service they and their clients had received once a referral was accepted for assessment and possible treatment.

The rationale for the project was further supported by the limited number of studies that have investigated the referral of learning-disabled clients to psychotherapy and psychological services (Waddell & Evers, 2000). Previous studies have generally focused on psychiatric consultations offered to people with learning disabilities and the relation between psychiatric diagnosis, referral reasons, and interventions outcomes (Khan, Cowan, & Roy, 1997; King, DeAntonio, McCracken, Forness, & Ackerland, 1994; Mansell, 1994). In addition, the questionnaires also aimed to gather information about how referrers established the client's consent to a referral for psychodynamic or psychoanalytic psychotherapy and, once they had consented, how clients were prepared for taking up an assessment as a result of a referral. An associate psychologist and one of the clinical psychologists in the Learning Disabilities Service undertook the survey.

Method

This survey aimed to target professionals who had referred clients to the Tavistock Learning Disabilities Service since it was established in 1995. A questionnaire was sent out to all those who had made a referral for an individual, a family, or a staff consultation. The questionnaire comprised scaled, open-ended, and multiple-choice questions. The questionnaire was divided into sections aiming to gain views and information about the reasons for which a referral had been made, how referrers gained their clients' consent to make the referral, and their views about the referral process they experienced.

Participants

All referrers were considered as possible participants, including those where the case was no longer open to the Learning Disabilities Service. Where the case was closed, this generally meant that the treatment had been completed. In some closed cases an assessment had been completed, and it had been concluded that a psychodynamic or psychoanalytic approach would not be best suited to the individual's needs. In all of these cases alternative recommendations had been made.

The majority of the participating referrers were GPs working either in single-handed practices or in health centres with several partners. Other referrers included professionals working as part of specialized teams in Social Services and Health Service learning disability teams or in Child and Family Services, in schools, or in residential units for adults with learning disabilities.

Results

Of the 176 questionnaires sent to referrers, only 13% were returned completed. Clearly the response to the questionnaire was extremely low, and therefore it was not possible to analyse the questionnaires quantitatively. Instead, questionnaires were analysed using qualitative methodology. Using a grounded theory approach (Henwood & Pidgeon, 1995), several common themes were identified and explored.

Referrers who answered the questionnaires came from a variety of professional backgrounds, including consultant psychiatrists specializing in learning disabilities and child psychiatry, social workers and residential social workers, consultant paediatricians, and clinical psychologists, head teachers, psychotherapists, counsellors, and community nurses. Only 17% of respondents were general practitioners. As GPs are the largest profession making referrals to the Learning Disabilities Service, the small number of responses from this group may help to explain the poor response rate overall.

Most of the respondents (65%) made one referral; the remaining referred up to three clients, with the exception of one respondent, who had made 10 referrals.

Why refer to the Learning Disabilities Service at the Tavistock?

The majority of the respondents stated that they referred to the Learning Disabilities Service at the Tavistock because they knew of the work of the team through colleagues. Others referred because they had heard about the team's work through conferences and published literature or from personal experience of working at the Tavistock Clinic. There was also evidence that leaflets about the Learning Disabilities Service and parental requests to referrers played a role in the referral being made to the team.

A motivating theme that emerged was the need to make a referral to a specialist psychotherapy service. A common element motivating referrals was cited as lack of expertise in local services. A number of reasons were given for making a referral to the Learning Disabilities Service in preference to local services, including the need for individual and long-term psychoanalytic treatment, shorter waiting list, and patient or parent preference for the Tavistock Clinic. Another frequent response was the suggestion that other models of treatment available to the referrer would not be successful in helping with the client's difficulties. Although most referrers did not specify which kind of patient they felt would not be able to use a psychodynamic approach, some 35% indicated that in their opinion severely learning-disabled service users who had serious difficulties with communication or aggressive behaviour, and those requiring an extensive outreach service, may be contraindicated in using this model of intervention.

Referrers were asked to tick boxes relating to the reasons they referred clients to the Learning Disabilities Service. The instructions required them to tick one or more boxes, and the results are illustrated in Figure 12.1. Emotional difficulties were the cited as the most frequent reason (78%) for referral, followed closely by behavioural problems (61%), and family issues (43.5%). Behaviour-management-related problems (35%) and abuse (22%) were also relatively frequent citations. Bereavement and transition-related difficulties were listed in 9% of responses and self-injurious behaviour and aggressive behaviour in only 4% of the questionnaires. "Other" reasons included difficulties around sexuality, difficulties at school, and parental problems.

Reasons for referrals

The types of intervention packages most frequently requested were individual therapy (74%) and assessment (70%). Family

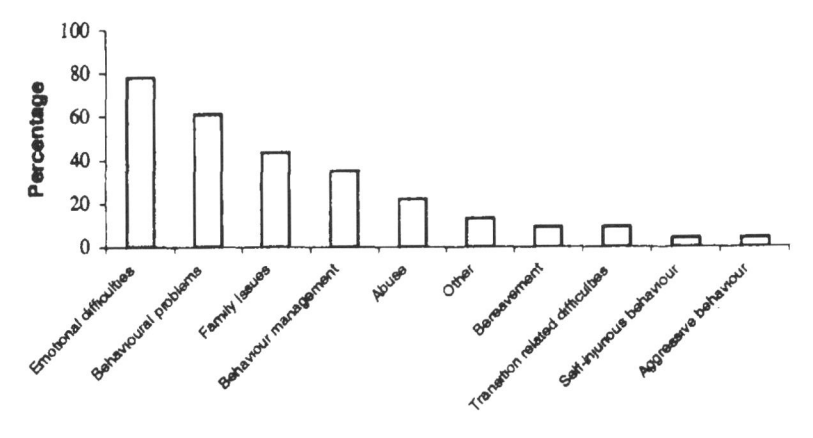

Figure 12.1

therapy and a multidisciplinary approach were requested in 44% of referrals, and consultation work in 9% of referrals.

In 35% of the questionnaires referrers stated that they had contacted other services—including psychiatric services, community teams for people with learning disabilities and other local services—before referring clients to the Learning Disabilities Service.

Consent to the referral

We were interested in how referrers gained consent for referrals and how they discussed the referral with clients before making it. In the responses returned, more than half (57%) of the clients referred were felt to have understood the reasons behind the referral, while almost a third were reported not to have understood the relevance of the referral.

Of the clients, 74% were reported to have consented to the referral to the Learning Disabilities Service; however, 22% of clients were reported not to have given consent, as their parents had sanctioned the referral. In many cases parents appeared to play a role in understanding the motivations for a referral and in giving their consent in addition to gaining consent from individuals.

The majority of clients were reported to have been prepared for the referral by the referrer giving an explanation of the intervention. However, on 26% of the questionnaires the referrer had left this section blank; it was therefore unclear how these clients had been prepared for the referral.

Over half of the responses stated that support staff and family members were positive and supportive of the referral being made; only 13% were clearly negative, and a further 13% were said to be ambivalent, unsure about the benefits a psychoanalytic model might bring, or they were reported to be difficult to involve in meetings.

The referral process

The Learning Disabilities Service wanted to ensure that their referrers felt that they were getting a high-quality service. The questionnaires included several questions related to the current referral process and the standards set for communication with referrers once a referral had been accepted, on completion of an assessment or when a treatment package had been offered. Referrers were given the opportunity to suggest improvements to the current processes. Over half the respondents rated the explanation they received of the process of assessment/treatment as good or very good. In addition, various ways to improve this aspect of the work were suggested. Some referrers stated that they would appreciate more printed information about the psychodynamic and psychoanalytic approach, about procedures such as reviews and arrangements or reasons for ending therapy. Others requested better communication and explanation about the individual assessment and its outcomes, including criteria for patients' suitability.

In 74% of questionnaires, communication between the referrer and the Learning Disabilities Service was rated as very good, good, or adequate. Respondents' suggestions to improve communication included increased telephone or written contact and more information about what the intervention would entail about the client's progress during interventions and possible waiting times.

Approximately half of the questionnaires rated the interim progress reports sent throughout the duration of the intervention as very good, good, or adequate. Some respondents said they did not receive any interim report, and some referrals were for assessment only and did not progress into a treatment package. This may explain the reduced number of ratings in this category.

The referral process was rated as very efficient or efficient by 56% of the respondents, and 22% said they had experienced the referral process as inefficient. About a quarter (22%) of respondents did not give views of the referral process. The reason for the absence of ratings is unclear.

About a third of respondents (35%) stated that their relationship with clients did not change after the referral. Some commented on the clients viewing their referrer as a link person, being confused about the lack of communication between professionals, and experiencing the referral as a rejection. One referrer suggested that following treatment, a client appeared to have gained a "new communicative vocabulary", had an increased ability to talk about themselves and an increased trust in staff, and had independently approached a service to ask for further counselling.

Issues resulting from clinical audit projects

These clinical audit projects have been very helpful in giving information to the service about performance. They generally suggest that the Learning Disabilities Service is providing a high-quality and a helpful service to the referrers and clients. There are, however, several issues that arise from the results of these two projects that can be explored in relation to the body of published literature relating to research and people with learning disabilities.

The low response to the referrer's questionnaire needs some exploration. There are several issues that may have influenced this lower-than-expected return rate. In the literature it is notable that other researchers concerned with learning disabilities services and the providing of psychotherapy obtained similarly low response rates (e.g. Nagel & Leiper, 1999, Waddell & Evers, 2000). The questionnaire was sent to all referrers who had ever referred a client to the Learning Disabilities Service. Some questionnaires were returned with information to say that the referrer had moved on from their job or was no longer known at the address where the questionnaire had been sent. It is possible that people who had been referred seven years ago and whose treatments had terminated were no longer so "alive" in the minds of the respondents. Alternatively, it is possible that those referrers were no longer in touch with the clients referred, or that they did not feel they had time to respond to a questionnaire about a service that they were no longer using.

It may also be relevant that many referrers cited that they had referred to the Learning Disabilities Service at the Tavistock because they had professional or personal links with the Clinic. The nature of the funding for our service relies on GP- or consultant-approved referrals, and therefore it is possible that those returning the questionnaire were the people with closer links to the Clinic and a desire to help ensure a high-quality service. Only 17% of questionnaires were returned by GP's; consultant psychiatrists, psychologists, and paediatricians made up a further 49% of the respondents. This raises the issue of how best to promote the Learning Disabilities Service.

The matter of consent in the referrers survey and the DNA rates in the audit report warrant some discussion. The issue of consent to a referral being made to the service and consent to treatment is complex and widely discussed in the literature. Arscott, Dagnan, and Stenfert-Kroese (1998) found that most subjects in a sample of 40 people with mild to severe learning disabilities had an understanding about the research project in which they were asked to participate; however, very few seemed to have a deeper comprehension of the effects the research might have in terms of benefits or risks, and very few were able to understand that they could refuse to participate if they wanted to do so. Acquiescence is well known as a problem in ensuring that people with learning disabilities make informed choices (Seligman & Budd, 1986; Seligman, Budd, Spanhel, & Schoenrock, 1981; Seligman, Budd, Winer, Schoenrock, & Martin, 1982; Simons, Booth, & Booth, 1989). It might follow that those clients for whom referrers were unsure about consent to the referral being made were also those clients who fell into the 31% who had not attended appointments once the Learning Disabilities Service had offered treatment. This issue clearly needs some attention. However, there is an increasing body of literature that explores effective methodologies for seeking and gaining informed consent for both research projects and treatment packages for people with learning disabilities that could be drawn on as a means of helping referrers to fully prepare clients for referrals made to our service (e.g. Atkinson, 1989; Booth & Booth, 1994; Chapman & Oakes, 1995).

One final issue that arises from the results of the referrers' survey is linked to a point that has been discussed in some of the clinical chapters in this book but has also been looked at in a wider context of work with people with learning disabilities. Most referrers stated that they hoped their clients would receive individual treatment packages of weekly psychotherapy sessions. This reflects the type of treatment packages most frequently offered following an assessment from the Learning Disabilities Service, which may explain the high percentage of satisfaction reported when asked about the referral process. There are very clear standards about the level of communication that will be adhered to by the Learning Disabilities Service, and these standards are discussed with referrers as part of the assessment procedure. However a quarter of respondents said they would have liked more information from the therapists about the progress of therapy, and they had expected regular telephone and written contact with the team. It is possible that those who were not satisfied with the level of communication between therapist and referrer were those respondents who would usually be very involved in their client's life and therefore found it hard to be excluded from the separated space of the treatment.

Outcome or process evaluation

In terms of formal methods of research into the effectiveness of treatments, there are two main areas of study to consider: outcome questions, which aim to find out whether the therapy approach has any positive impact (for instance, does it work?) alternatively, researchers may wish to pose process questions, which explore which aspects of therapy are causing any changes (for instance, how does it work?).

Both types of questions are important for developing appropriate research designs, but they require quite different methods of investigation. Outcome studies tend to take a baseline measurement before the treatment starts and a repeat measurement once the treatment has finished. More comprehensive outcome studies take repeat measures at regular intervals during treatment and may include follow-ups after the treatment has ended to establish maintenance of the changes measured. The methods of measurement tend to take the form of standardized assessments, interviews, and questionnaires. Outcome studies tend to produce numerical, *quantitative* data and therefore cannot give us much information about the quality of interactions or relationships or the method used by treatments that are working—or not working, as the case may be.

Process studies explore in detail the content of treatment, commonly using transcripts from video- or tape-recorded sessions, so that the impact of aspects of treatment on the clients and vice versa can be explored. It is then possible to explore in detail the elements of treatment, such as the impact of an interpretation or a challenge to a defence, by looking at the responses and correlates, including verbal and physical—movement, facial expression—behaviours. These studies are very time-consuming and tend to be limited to smaller sample sizes; they also tend to produce subtle, unquantifiable findings that are referred to as *qualitative* data.

Some studies combine the two types of investigation—so the relationship between the process and the outcome is studied, for example, by aspects of treatment being altered and the impact on outcome being explored. Such studies may draw on both qualitative and quantitative methods of data collection.

In deciding what type of data will be collected, a decision needs to be made about what information is being sought—hence the importance of generating research questions and aims before designing the study. This may sound like an obvious point, but it is often missed in the enthusiasm of getting going with data collection. There are many factors that need to be taken into account, such as time and financial constraints, numbers of participants, availability of controls, access to equipment such as tests or assessment schedules, video and audio equipment, as well as ethical considerations. The careful planning of a research project is the most critical stage of the process. There are many good texts on designing research projects that the reader can access—for example, those by Barker, Pistrang, and Elliott (1995) and Parry and Watts (1996).

General issues in psychotherapy outcome research

Roth and Fonagy (1995) completed a large-scale review of published papers concerning the efficacy and effectiveness of various types of psychotherapies for the Department of Health. They noted that there is an enormous number of outcome studies already published, and new publications are emerging at a rate of about 50 a month (Fonagy, 1995). However, evidence specifically about psychodynamic therapy is inconsistent. There are numerous difficulties in making comparisons of studies, because different treatment methods and data collection methods are employed. Roth and Fonagy suggest that *randomized control trials* are the most stringent and most likely to identify a causal relationship between the intervention and any improvement. Randomized control trials are those that compare a treatment group with a group matched to the subjects in treatment who are either receiving a different type of treatment or no treatment (e.g. are on a waiting list). Although a robust research method, such trials generate numerous difficulties in setting up. Fonagy and Higgit (1989) have identified several of these issues that include concerns about the ethics of using placebo treatments in medical research when an effective treatment has already been identified, and that in studies comparing different treatments the models being compared may have different intensity and duration, making "like-for-like" comparison extremely difficult.

Fonagy (1995) suggests that studies to evaluate the effectiveness of psychotherapeutic interventions should ensure that they include measures relating to the patient's view of any changes that have occurred, the therapist's view, and the views of other people in the patient's network in addition to standardized measures of change.

Outcome studies of therapeutic approaches with people with learning disabilities

Published outcome studies of psychoanalytic or psychodynamic psychotherapy are relatively sparse. This is partly a consequence of very few services offering this type of intervention, but it can also be linked to the specific issues and difficulties that arise when conducting research with people with learning disabilities.

There are two papers that review the significant research related to outcome and psychotherapy in the field of learning disability (Beail, 1995; Hurley, 1989). They both highlight the fact that most studies describe single case studies that explore issues of technique and the tasks of therapy. Most show improvement in the person's psychological well-being over time but use subjective measures of change rather than robust standardized measures (Emanuel, 1997; Sinason, 1992b; Stokes, 1992; Symington, 1981).

Beail and Warden (1996) published an account of a comprehensive evaluation of a psychodynamic psychotherapy service. They adapted self-report tools that aim to measure changes in self-esteem and psychological symptoms to monitor the effect of weekly individual psychodynamic psychotherapy on 10 people with learning disabilities. Their participants were aged between 18 and 49 years and attended between 5 and 48 sessions with their therapist. Measures were administered before the intervention commenced, at intervals of 8 sessions, at termination of therapy, and at three months following the end of therapy. The results suggested improvements in self-esteem and reductions in reported psychological symptoms. In a later study, Beail (1998) reported a reduction in aggression in 25 male participants who had been referred for behaviour difficulties through a forensic service. Behavioural measures were used to record difficult behaviour before treatment commenced, at termination of therapy, and at a six-month follow-up.

In a previous study undertaken at the Tavistock Clinic, Bichard, Sinason, and Usiskin (1996) showed changes in projective measures (Goodenough-Harris Draw-a-Person test—Harris, 1963) in eight people with learning disabilities being offered individual psychotherapy from a psychodynamic perspective. The study highlights the distinction Sinason (1992b) and her colleagues have made between cognitive intelligence and emotional intelligence or the individual's ability to relate to other people, to think, and to gain insight into difficulties they are experiencing. The study looks at changes in cognitive measures and in developments in therapy through collecting qualitative reports from the participants, the therapists, and a significant person in the patient's network. Although unpublished, these results suggest that improvements in emotional intelligence may have influenced changes in scores on the cognitive measures. The group in treatment showed some improvement on test scores when compared with a control group.

Frankish (1989) published an outcome report on psychoanalytical psychotherapy treatment of seven intellectually disabled children and adults. Descriptions of the participants' behaviour before and after the treatment were analysed. In the seven cases, the problem behaviour was reduced, but only in one case was it eliminated; follow-up data were not collected, and therefore it is not possible to speculate on the permanence of these changes.

Skene (1991) used repertory grids (based on Kelly's Psychology of Personal Constructs, 1977), Anthony and Bene's Family Relation Test, and the Bell Adjustment Inventory (1957) to measure improvements in emotional adjustment and changes in choice of personal constructs in six people with mild learning disabilities attending group psychotherapy. The results were compared with scores on the same measures of a control group attending another day centre. Skene also interviewed care staff supporting the group members in their day services. The qualitative results suggested that the group had been helpful to the participants. They felt they had been given an opportunity to air grievances and had developed a greater sense of optimism and autonomy. Staff reported that the group members had become more introspective and more cautious in new situations, but that one group member had become more withdrawn. The overall impression of the carers was that the group had expanded the members' personality boundaries, but as the research was time-limited there had been little evidence of behaviour changes. There was a recommendation that the group should continue. Qualitative results showed significant improvement on the Bell Adjustment Inventory, which suggests that the therapy effectively ameliorated emotional adjustment. The changes in Personal Construct Repertory Grids showed that participants had expanded on their constructs relating to self-confidence, happiness, and aggression, suggesting that they had gained some insight into the difficulties they were experiencing. The participants in the therapy group also indicated a need to change themselves and to investigate issues realign to cause and effect of difficulties.

Outcome research project

As stated in the introduction to this chapter, the Tavistock Learning Disabilities Service is currently undertaking an outcome study to measure the effectiveness of the treatment offered to clients.

The research focuses on the developments that take place through the process of once-weekly long-term psychotherapy (at least a year in length), with each psychotherapy session lasting for 50 minutes. The aim of the therapy is to provide the client with a greater understanding of his or her internal world and particularly of processes relating to interpersonal relationships. It is expected that as a result of increased insight, clients will be in a better position to adjust to the reality of the limitations they experience and sustain positive and lasting relationships with others.

Following discussion with therapists and through careful analysis of the literature relating to psychotherapy (both with the general population and with people with learning disabilities), we considered that demonstrable signs that a person was achieving a greater understanding of their internal world and relationships would be: the ability to form more stable relationships, improved social adaptiveness, a greater grounding in reality, greater curiosity about their environment, and an improved ability to express themselves. We would not necessarily expect a shift in cognitive ability or a major reduction in the original symptomatology, although such positive changes have been observed both in our clinical experience and in other outcome research studies (e.g.

Bichard, Sinason, & Usiskin, 1996, and the Beail studies described above).

Several studies have explored the outcome of psychotherapy before, as seen above; however, this current research project has aimed to broaden the focus of research to take account of cognitive factors, personality, adaptive behaviour measures, and any changes in symptomatology. The research project has been designed to follow three distinct phases:

In Phase 1 the aim has been to collect preliminary data for all participants during the course of treatment and to collate the data, with the aim of applying for funding for a research assistant. Once funding has been secured, the research assistant will be expected to embark on Phase 2 and to extend the number of participants undertaking assessment and treatment from the Learning Disabilities Service.

In Phases 1 and 2 all clients assessed for individual psychotherapy and subsequently accepted for treatment by the Learning Disabilities Service will be contacted and asked whether they would like to participate in the research project. The inclusion criteria for the treatment group would be those people aged 18 and above, with an IQ of between 50 and 69, who have been offered and have accepted treatment for a minimum of one year. Each client who consents to participate in the research will be invited to attend a separate appointment with team member other than the therapist to undertake a number of assessments that make up the dependent and independent measures of the research design. This appointment will take place post-assessment but prior to treatment packages commencing. At the end of each year of treatment the projective and inventory scales will be repeated, and at the end of therapy all measures, including cognitive assessments, will be repeated.

Individual measures to be used include cognitive assessments: WAIS-III-UK, the Bender Gestalt Test, projective assessments; Object Relations test, Draw-a-Person test, and the Kinetic Family Drawing, an adaptation of the Brief Symptom Inventory and repertory grid measures (Burns & Kaufman, 1970). Therapists' ratings will be recorded by ensuring that the clinician working with each client completes a brief questionnaire following each session that focuses on areas where change might be envisaged, such as relatedness, level of functioning, and countertransference responses. An adult who is familiar with the client, such as a family member or keyworker, will complete the Vineland Adaptive Behaviour Scales.

Due to the relatively small numbers of people who are likely to fulfil the inclusion criteria, it is envisaged that 4 to 6 participants will be recruited each year; it is hoped that there will be 15 participants over the three-year period of the study.

In Phase 3 a control group will be recruited, and their development or changes in the specified domains of functioning will be compared to the treatment group (those participants recruited from Phase 1 and 2) This will enable us to make more precise statements about the impact of psychotherapeutic psychotherapy on adults with learning disabilities. We do not think that there is an equivalent treatment group who would act as an effective control group, and therefore ideally we would recruit a group as a non-treatment control group.

Currently Phase 1 of the outcome research project is underway, and we have recruited 6 participants this year.

Conclusions

This chapter has aimed to illustrate the how the Tavistock Clinic Learning Disabilities Service continues to try to ensure that a high-quality, effective service is provided to the recipients, the referrers, and those supporting the individual service users. The audit projects have given valuable information that has informed our practice and helped us to develop clear and appropriate standards of practice. The referrers' survey has offered useful feedback that has enabled us to think about the referral process and about effective communication with other agencies. The DNA audit has given us an opportunity to explore some of the difficulties that the client group might experience in accessing a specialist psychoanalytic psychotherapy service. The ongoing outcome research project has afforded an exciting opportunity to think about the effectiveness of psychoanalytic psychotherapy for people with learning disabilities in the context of a growing body of literature. We are looking forward to moving on with the project and to analysing the results. It is hoped that this project will not only ensure a high quality and effective service to clients but will, in addition, make a valuable contribution to the published literature and encourage others to offer a psychoanalytic approach.

REFERENCES

Allen, P., Pahl, J., & Quine, L. (1990). *Care Staff in Transition: The Impact on Staff of Changing Services for People with Mental Handicaps.* London: HMSO.

Altschuler, J. (1997). *Working with Chronic Illness.* London: Macmillan.

Alvarez, A. (1992). *Live Company.* London/New York: Tavistock, Routledge.

Anthony, E. J., & Bene, E. (1957). A technique for the objective assessment of the child's family relationships. *Journal of Mental Science, 103*: 541–555.

Arscott, K., Dagnan, D., & Stenfert-Kroese, B. (1998). Consent to psychological research by people with an intellectual disability. *Journal of Applied Research in Intellectual Disabilities 11* (1): 77–83.

Atkinson, D. (1988). Research interviews with people with mental handicaps. *Mental Handicap Research 1* (1): 75–90.

Atkinson, D. (1989). *Someone to Turn to: The Social Worker's Role and the Role of Front Line Staff in Relation to People with Mental Handicaps.* Kidderminster: British Institute of Mental Handicap Publications.

Atkinson, L., Scott, B., Chrisholm, V., & Blackwell, J. (1995). Cognitive coping, affective distress and maternal sensitivity: Mothers of children with Down Syndrome. *Developmental Psychology, 33*: 668–676.

Barker, C., Pistrang, N., & Elliott, R. (1995). *Research Methods in Clinical and Counselling Psychology*. Chichester: Wiley.

Beail, N. (1995). Outcome of psychoanalysis, psychoanalytic and psychodynamic psychotherapy with people with intellectual disabilities: A review. *Changes, 13*: 186–191.

Beail, N. (1998). Psychoanalytic psychotherapy with men with intellectual disabilities: A preliminary outcome study. *British Journal of Medical Psychology, 71*: 1–11.

Beail, N., & Warden, S. (1996). Evaluation of a psychodynamic psychotherapy service for adults with intellectual disabilities: Rationale, design and preliminary outcome data. *Journal of Applied Research in Intellectual Disabilities, 9* (3): 223–228.

Bentovim, A. (1972). Emotional disturbances of handicapped pre-school children and their families: Attitudes to the child. *British Medical Journal, 3*: 579–581.

Bentovim, A. (1975). The impact of malformation on the emotional development of the child and his family. In: C. L. Berry & D. E. Poswillo (Eds.), *Teratology: Trends and Application* (pp. 223–233). Berlin: Springer-Verlag.

Bichard, S. H., Sinason, V., & Usiskin, J. (1996). Measuring change in mentally retarded clients in long-term psychoanalytic psychotherapy, 1: The draw-a-person test. *NADD Newsletter, 13* (5): 6–11.

Bick, E. (1967). The experiences of the skin in early object relations. In: *Collected Papers of Martha Harris and Esther Bick*. London: Roland Harris Education Trust.

Bion, W. R. (1961). *Experiences in Groups and Other Papers*. New York: Basic Books.

Bion, W. R. (1962a). *Learning from Experience*. London: Heinemann. Reprinted London: Karnac, 1984.

Bion, W. R. (1962b). A theory of thinking. *International Journal of Psychoanalysis, 43*, 306–310. In: *Second Thoughts*. London: Karnac, 1984. Also in: *Melanie Klein Today, Vol. 1*. London: Routledge, 1988.

Bion, W. R. (1967a). On hallucination. In: *Second Thoughts*. London: Karnac, 1984.

Bion, W. R. (1967b). *Second Thoughts*. London: Karnac, 1984.

Booth, T., & Booth, W. (1994). The use of depth interviews with vulnerable subjects: Lessons from a research study of parents with learning disabilities. *Society, Science and Medicine, 49* (3): 415–424.

Boston, M., & Szur, R. (Eds.) (1983). *Psychotherapy with Severely Deprived Children*. London: Routledge & Kegan Paul.
Bowlby, J. (1979). *The Making and Breaking of Affectional Bonds*. London: Tavistock.
Braten, S. (1987). Dialogic mind: The infant and the adult in proto conversation. In: M. Carvallo (Ed.), *Nature, Cognition and Systems*. Dordrecht/Boston: D. Reidel.
Brazelton, T. B., Kosalowski, B., & Main, M. (1974). The origins of reciprocity: The early mother–infant interaction. In: M. Lewis & L. A. Rosenblum (Eds.), *The Effect of the Infant on Its Caregiver*. New York: Wiley.
Britton, R. (1989). The missing link: Parental sexuality in the Oedipus complex. In: R. Britton, M. Feldman, & E. O'Shaughnessy (Eds.), *The Oedipus Complex Today: Clinical Implications*. London: Karnac.
Britton, R. (1998). *Belief and Imagination: Explorations in Psychoanalysis*. London: Routledge.
Broucek, F. (1979). Efficacy in infancy: A review of some experimental studies and their possible implications of clinical theory. *International Journal of Psycho-Analysis*, 60: 311–316.
Burns, R. C., & Kaufman, S. H. (1970). *Kinetic Family Drawings (K-F-D): An Introduction to Understanding Children through Kinetic Drawings*. Oxford: Brunner/Mazel.
Cameron, S. J., Snowdon, A., & Orr, R. R. (1992). Emotional experiences by mothers of children with developmental disabilities. *Children's Health Care*, 21: 96–102.
Campbell, B. (2003). Sisters of no mercy. *The Guardian Weekend*, 12 April.
Chapman, K., & Oakes, P. (1995). Asking people with learning disabilities their views on direct psychological interventions. *Clinical Psychology Forum*, 81: 28–33.
Chappell, A. L. (1994). A question of friendship: Community care and the relationships of people with learning difficulties. *Disability and Society*, 9: 419–434.
Clegg, J. A., Standen, P. J., & Jones, G. (1996). Striking the balance: A grounded theory analysis of staff perspectives. *British Journal of Clinical Psychology*, 35: 249–264.
Davenhill, R., & Patrick, M. (1998). *Rethinking Clinical Audit: The Case of Psychotherapy Services in the NHS*. London: Routledge.

Dubinsky, A. (1997). Theoretical overview: The apprehension of emotional experience. In: M. Rustin, M. Rhode, A. Dubinsky, & H. Dubinsky (Eds.), *Psychotic States in Children*. London: Duckworth.

Emanuel, L. (1997). Facing the damage together: Some reflections arising from the treatment in psychotherapy of a severely mentally handicapped child. *Journal of Child Psychotherapy*, 23 (2): 279–302.

Emanuel, R. (1984). Primary disappointment. *Journal of Child Psychotherapy*, 10 (1): 71–87.

Emanuel, R. (1990). Psychotherapy with hospitalised children with leukaemia: Is it possible? *Journal of Child Psychotherapy*, 16 (2): 21–38.

Emerson, P. (1977). Covert grief reaction in mentally retarded clients. *Mental Retardation*, 15: 46–47.

Evans, J. (1998). *Active Analytic Group Therapy for Adolescents*. London: Jessica Kingsley.

Faerstein, L. M. (1986). Coping and defense mechanisms of mothers of learning disabled children. *Journal of Learning Disabilities*, 19: 8–11.

Firth, H. (1986). *A Move to the Community: Social Contact and Behaviour*. Unpublished manuscript, Northumberland Health Authority District Psychology Service, Morpeth, England.

Firth, H., & Rapley, M. (1990). *From Acquaintance to Friendship: Issues for People with Learning Disabilities*. Kidderminster: British Institute of Mental Handicap Publications.

Firth-Cozens, J. (1993). *Audit in Mental Health Services*. Hove: Erlbaum.

Flynn, M. C. (1989). *Independent Living for Adults with Mental Handicap: A Place of My Own*. London: Cassell.

Fonagy, P. (1995). Is there an answer to the outome reseach question: Waiting for Godot. *Changes*, 13.

Fonagy, P., & Higgit, A. (1989). Evaluating the performance of departments of psychiatry. *Journal of Psychoanalytic Psychotherapy*, 4: 121–153.

Frankish, P. (1989). Meeting the emotional needs of handicapped people: A psychodynamic approach. *Journal of Mental Deficiency Research*, 33: 407–414.

Fredman, G., & Dalal, C. (1998). Ending discourses: Implications for relationships and actions in therapy. *Human Systems: The Journal of Systemic Consultation and Management*, 9: 1–13.

Freud, S. (1909d). Notes upon a case of obsessional neurosis. *S.E.*, 10.

Freud, S. (1911b). Formulations on two principles of mental functioning. *S.E., 12*.
Freud, S. (1916–17). *Introductory Lectures on Psycho-Analysis*. *S.E., 16*.
Freud, S. (1917e). Mourning and melancholia. *S.E., 14*.
Freud, S. (1930a). *Civilization and Its Discontents* London: Penguin Edition.
Gorell-Barnes, G. (2002). *Getting It Right, Getting It Wrong: Developing an Internal Discourse about Ethnicity and Difference*. London: Karnac.
Harper, D. C., & Wadsworth, J. S. (1993). Grief in adults with mental retardation: Preliminary findings. *Research in Developmental Disabilities, 14*: 313–330.
Harris, D. (1963). *Goodenough-Harris Draw-a-Person Test*. New York: Harcourt Brace.
Haviland, J. (1976). Looking smart: The relationship between affect and intelligence in infancy. In: M. Lewis (Ed.), *Origins of Intelligence in Infancy and Early Childhood*. New York/London: Plenum Press.
Henwood, K., & Pidgeon, N. (1995). Grounded theory: A psychological research. *The Psychologist, 8*: 115–119.
Hernandez, I., Hodges, S., Miller, L., & Simpson, T. D. (2000). A psychotherapy service for children and adults with learning disability at the Tavistock Clinic, London. *British Journal of Learning Disabilities, 28*: 120–124.
Hobson, R. P. (1993a). The emotional origins of interpersonal understanding. *Philosophical Psychology, 6*: 227–249.
Hobson, R. P. (1993b). Perceiving attitudes, conceiving minds. In: C. Lewis & P. Mitchell (Eds.), *Origins of an Understanding of Mind*. Hillsdale, NJ: Lawrence Erlbaum Associates.
Hobson, R. P. (1993c). Understanding persons: The role of affect. In: S. Baron-Cohen, H. Tager-Flusberg, & D. Cohen (Eds.), *Understanding Other Minds: Perspectives from Autism*. Oxford: Oxford University Press.
Hodges, S. R. (2003). *Counselling Adults with Learning Disabilities Book*. Basingstoke: Palgrave, Macmillan.
Hoxter, S. (1983). Some feelings aroused in working with severely deprived children. In: M. Boston & R. Szur (Eds.), *Psychotherapy with Severely Deprived Children*. London: Routledge & Kegan Paul.

Hoxter, S. (1986). The significance of trauma in the difficulties encountered by physically disabled children. *Journal of Child Psychotherapy*, 12 (1): 87–103.

Hunter, M. (2001). *Psychotherapy with Young People in Care*. Hove: Brunner-Routledge.

Hurley, A. D. (1989). Individual psychotherapy with mentally retarded individuals: A review and call for research. *Research in Developmental Disabilities*, 10: 261–275.

Kelly, G. A. (1977). Personal construct theory and the psychotherapeutic interview. *Cognitive Therapy & Research* 1 (4): 355–362.

Khan, A., Cowan, C., & Roy, A. (1997). Personality disorders in people with learning disabilities: A community survey. *Journal of Intellectual Disability Research*, 41 (4): 324–330.

King, B. H., DeAntonio, C., McCracken. J. T., Forness S. R., & Ackerland, V. (1994). Psychiatric consultation in severe and profound mental retardation. *American Journal of Psychiatry*, 151 (12): 1802–1808.

Klein, M. (1928). Early stages of the Oedipus complex. In: *The Writings of Melanie Klein, Vol. 1: Love, Guilt and Reparation*. London: Hogarth Press, 1975.

Klein, M. (1935). A contribution to the psychogenesis of manic-depressive states. In: *The Writings of Melanie Klein, Vol. 1: Love, Guilt and Reparation*. London: Hogarth Press, 1975.

Klein, M. (1940). Mourning and its relation to manic-depressive states. In: *The Writings of Melanie Klein, Vol. 1: Love, Guilt and Reparation*. London: Hogarth Press, 1975.

Klein, M. (1946). Notes on some schizoid mechanisms. In: *The Writings of Melanie Klein, Vol. 3: Envy and Gratitude and Other Works*. London: Hogarth Press, 1975.

Krause, I.-B. (2002). *Uncertainty, Risk-taking and Ethics in Psychotherapy*. London: Karnac.

Lacan, J. (1977). *Écrits: A Selection*. London: Tavistock.

Mansell, J. (1994). The challenge of providing high-quality services. In: N. Bouras (Ed.), *Mental Health in Mental Retardation: Recent Advances and Practices*, 16: 328–340.

Mattison, V., & Pistrang, N. (2000). *Saying Goodbye: When Keyworker Relationships End*. London: Free Association Books.

McCormack, B. (1991). Thinking, discourse and the denial of history:

Psychodynamic aspects of mental handicap. *Irish Journal of Psychological Medicine, 8*: 59–64.

Meltzer, D. (1975a). Adhesive identification. *Contemporary Psychoanalysis, 2* (3).

Meltzer, D. (1975b). Dimensionality in mental functioning. In: *Explorations in Autism*. Strath Tay: Clunie Press.

Meltzer, D. (1988). On aesthetic reciprocity. In D. Meltzer & M. Harris Williams, *The Apprehension of Beauty* (pp. 42–58). Strath Tay: Clunie Press.

Meltzer, D. (1992). *The Claustrum: An Investigation of Claustrophobic Phenomena*. Strath Tay: Clunie Press.

Menzies, I. E. P. (1970). *The Functioning of Social Systems as a Defence against Anxiety*. London: Tavistock Institute of Human Relations.

Miller, L., Rustin, M., Rustin, M., & Shuttleworth, J. (1997). *Closely Observed Infants*. London: Duckworth.

Money-Kyrle, R. (1968). Cognitive development. In: *The Collected Papers of Roger Money-Kyrle*. Aberdeen: Aberdeen University Press, for Clunie Press, Roland Harris Educational Trust.

Muir, E. (1992). Watching, waiting, wondering: Applying psychoanalytic principles to mother–infant intervention. *Infant Mental Health Journal, 13* (4): 319–334.

Murray, L. (1991). Intersubjectivity, object relations theory and empirical evidence from mother–infant interactions. *Infant Mental Health Journal, 12*: 219–232.

Murray, L. (1992). The impact of maternal depression. *Journal of Child Psychiatry and Psychology, 33* (3).

Nagel, B., & Leiper R. (1999). A national survey of psychotherapy with people with learning disabilities. *Clinical Psychology Forum, 129*: 14–18.

Nitsun, M. (1989). Early development: Linking the individual and the group. *Group Analysis 22* (3): 249–261.

O'Shaughnessy, E. (1964). The absent object. *Journal of Child Psychotherapy, 1* (2): 34–43.

O'Shaughnessy, E. (1981). W. R. Bion's theory of thinking and new techniques in child analysis. In: *Melanie Klein Today, Vol. 2*. London: Routledge, 1988.

O'Shaughnessy, E. (1999). Relating to the super-ego. *International Journal of Psycho-Analysis, 80*: 861–870.

Oswin, M. (1981). *Bereavement and Mentally Handicapped People. Discussion Paper.* London: King's Fund.
Oswin, M. (1991). *Am I Allowed to Cry? A Study of Bereavement amongst People with Learning Difficulties.* London: Condor.
Papadopoulos, R. (2001). Refugee families: Issues of systemic supervision. *Journal of Family Therapy*, 24 (4): 405–422.
Papadopoulos, R. (2002). *Therapeutic Care for Refugees: No Place like Home.* London: Karnac.
Parry, G., & Watts, F. N. (1996). *Behavioural and Mental Health Research: A Handbook of Skills and Methods.* Hove: Erlbaum.
Reid, S. (1999). The assessment of the child with autism: A family perspective. In: A. Alvarez & S. Reid (Eds.), *Autism and Personality: Findings from the Tavistock Autism Workshop.* London/New York: Routledge.
Rhode, M. (1999). Echo or answer? The move towards ordinary speech in three children with autistic spectrum disorder. In: A. Alvarez & S. Reid (Eds.), *Autism and Personality: Findings from the Tavistock Autism Workshop.* London: Routledge.
Rosenberg, M. L. (1990). Disability and the personal–professional connection. In: B. Genevau & R. S. Katz (Eds.), *Countertransference and Older Adults* (pp. 69–79). London: Sage.
Roth, A., & Fonagy, P. (1995). *What Works for Whom?* London: HMSO.
Rycroft, C. (1968). *A Critical Dictionary of Psychoanalysis.* London: Nelson.
Seligman, C. K., & Budd, E. C. (1986). Pictures as an aid in questioning mentally retarded persons. *Rehabilitation Counselling Bulletin*, 29: 175–181.
Seligman, C. K., Budd, E. C., Spanhel, C. L., & Schoenrock, C. J. (1981). Asking questions of retarded persons: A comparison of yes/no and either/or formats. *Applied Research in Mental Retardation*, 2: 347–357.
Seligman, C. K., Budd, E. C., Winer, J. L., Schoenrock, C. J., & Martin, R. W. (1982). Evaluating alternative techniques of questioning mentally retarded persons. *American Journal of Mental Deficiency*, 86: 511–518.
Simons, K., Booth, T., & Booth, W. (1989). Speaking out: User studies and people with learning disabilities. *Policy, Research and Planning* 7 (1): 9–17.

Sinason, V. (1986). Secondary mental handicap and its relationship to trauma. *Psychoanalytic Psychotherapy*, 2 (2): 131–154.

Sinason, V. (1992a). Finding meaning without words. In: *Mental Handicap and the Human Condition: New Approaches from the Tavistock*. London: Free Association Books.

Sinason, V. (1992b). *Mental Handicap and the Human Conditions: New Approaches from the Tavistock*. London: Free Association Books.

Sinason, V. (1992c). Primary and secondary handicap. In: *Mental Handicap and the Human Condition*. London: Free Association Books.

Sinason, V., & Stokes, J. (1992). Secondary mental handicap as a defence. In: A. Waitman & S. Conboy-Hill (Eds), *Psychotherapy and Mental Handicap*. London: Sage.

Skene, R. A. (1991). Towards a measure of psychotherapy in mental handicap. *British Journal of Mental Subnormality*, 37 (2): 101–110.

Spillius, E. B. (1988). *Melanie Klein Today*. London: Routledge.

Steiner, J. (1992). *Psychic Retreats*. London/New York: Routledge.

Stern, D. N. (1977). *The First Relationship: Infant and Mother*. London: Fontana.

Stern, D. N. (1983). Schemas of affective experience of self with other. In: J. Lichtenberg & S. Kaplan (Eds.), *Reflections on Self Psychology*. Hillsdale, NJ: Analytic Press.

Stern, D. N. (1985). *The Interpersonal World of the Infant*. New York: Basic Books.

Stokes, J. (1987). "Insights from Psychotherapy". Paper presented at International Symposium on Mental Handicap, Royal Society of Medicine, 25 February.

Stokes, J. (1992). Secondary mental handicap as a defence. In: A. Waitman & S. Conboy-Hill (Eds.), *Psychotherapy and Mental Handicap* (pp. 46–58). London: Sage.

Symington, N. (1981). The psychotherapy of a subnormal patient. *British Journal of Medical Psychology*, 54: 187–199.

Symington, N. (1986). *The Analytic Experience: Lectures from the Tavistock*. London: Free Association Books.

Terry, P. (1997). *Counselling the Elderly and Their Carers*. London: Macmillan.

Trevarthen, C. (1977). Descriptive analyses of infant communicative behaviour. In: H. R. Schaffer (Ed.), *Studies in Mother–Infant Interaction*. London: Academic Press.

Trevarthen, C. (1980). Foundations of intersubjectivity: Development of interpersonal and cooperative understanding in infants. In: D. Olson (Ed.), *The Social Foundations of Language and Thought*. New York: W. W. Norton.

Tronick, E. (1989). Emotions and emotional communication in infants. *American Psychologist* (February): 112–119.

Tustin, E. (1983). Thoughts on autism with special reference to a paper by Melanie Klein. *Journal of Child Psychotherapy*, 9: 119–131.

Waddell, H., & Evers, C. (2000). Psychological services for people with learning disabilities living in the community: Focus group views. *Clinical Psychology Forum*, 141: 34–38.

Waddell, M. (1998). *Inside Lives: Psychoanalysis and the Development of the Personality*. London: Duckworth. Reprinted London: Karnac, 2002.

Waitman, A., & Conboy-Hill, S. (1992). *Psychology and Mental Handicap*. London: Sage.

Wallace, W. (2000). "National/London Learning Disability Strategy." Paper presented at the conference of the Psychologists' Special Interest Group in Learning Disabilities, Abergavenny, Wales.

Williams, G. (1997). Thinking and learning in deprived children. In: *Internal Landscapes and Foreign Bodies*. London: Duckworth.

Winnicott, D. W. (1960). The theory of the parent–infant relationship. In: D. W. Winnicott (Ed.), *The Maturational Processes and the Facilitating Environment*. London: Hogarth Press.

Yanok, J., & Beifus, J. A. (1993). Communicating about loss and mourning: Death education for individuals with mental retardation. *Mental Retardation*, 31: 144–147.

INDEX

abandonment, effects of, 113
abnormal superego, 84
abuse, xxiv, 44, 53, 113, 134, 146, 172
   drug, 113
   physical, 2, 36
   sexual, 2, 35, 36, 53, 54, 59, 64, 113
Ackerland, V., 170
adhesive identification, 56
adolescents, therapeutic work with, xxiv
adults, therapeutic work with, xxiv
aesthetic experience, 57
"aesthetic reciprocity", 47–49, 68
Allen, P., 151, 155
alpha:
   elements, 115–116
   function, 115, 117, 121, 144
Altschuler, J., 24
Alvarez, A., 58
"Andrew" [clinical example], 16–29
"Andy" [clinical example], 139–140
Anthony, E. J., 181

anxieties, primitive, 116, 123, 130–131
Arscott, K., 176
Atkinson, D., 152, 177
Atkinson, L., 116
attachment:
   failure of, 45
   formation, 3
   keyworkers to resident patients, 156
   mother, to handicapped or damaged baby, xxv, 47–68
   patients' need for, 152, 163, 166
   theory, 18
attendance audit, 168–169
"Audrey" [clinical example], 157, 160
autism, 58, 70
autistic children, work with, xxii
autistic defence(s), 53–56
autistic traits, 49, 56
autistic-type states of withdrawal, 46

INDEX

Baikie, A., xiii, xxv, 98–111
Bangladeshi Service, Tavistock Clinic, 31
Barker, C., 179
Beail, N., xxi, 180, 183
"Beatrice" [clinical example], 93–95
Beifus, J. A., 163
Bell Adjustment Inventory, 181, 182
"Bella" [clinical example], 128–131
Bells's Adjustment Inventory, 182
Bender Gestalt Test, 183
Bene, E., 181
Bentovim, A., 142
bereavement, 163, 172
beta elements, 115
Bichard, S. H., xxi, 31, 180, 183
Bick, E., 54, 63
"Bill" [clinical example], 160–161
Bion, W. R., 6, 62
   alpha elements/function, 115
   beta elements, 115
   containment, model of, 16, 18, 46, 96, 123
   ego-destructive superego, concept of, 84
   "group basic assumption", 22, 27
   "K", concept of, 47, 95, 96, 98
   learning from experience, 72
   on linking, 123
   mother–infant interactions, 114
      maternal containment, xxv, 16, 46
      maternal reverie, 115
   "nameless dread", 115, 123
   projective identification, 143, 144
   on thinking, 12, 74, 115, 123
Blackwell, J., 116
body, knowledge of, 135–137
Booth, T., 176, 177
Booth, W., 176, 177
borderline personality disorder, 70
Boston, M., 3
Bowlby, J., 18
Braten, S., 144
Brazelton, T. B., 143, 144
breast, good, 96

Brief Symptom Inventory, 183
Britton, R., xxv, 112, 115
Broucek, F., 143
Budd, E. C., 176
"Buna" [clinical example], 99–111
Burns, R. C., 183

Cameron, S. J., 116
Campbell, B., 36
catastrophic anxiety, 26, 28
"Catherine" [clinical example], 159
Chapman, K., 177
Chappell, A. L., 152
children:
   with terminal physical illnesses and learning disabilities, work with, xxiv, 14–29
   therapeutic work with, xxiv
Chrisholm, V., 116
Cioeta, M., xiii–xiv, xxvi, 167–185
"Claudia" [clinical example (Meltzer)], 48–49, 58
claustrum, 8
Clegg, J. A., 155
clinical audit, Tavistock Clinic learning disabilities service, xxvi, 167–185
clinical examples:
   "Andrew", 16–29
   "Andy", 139–140
   "Audrey", 157, 160
   "Beatrice", 93–95
   "Bella", 128–131
   "Bill", 160–161
   "Buna", 99–111
   "Catherine", 159
   "Claudia" [Meltzer], 48–49, 58
   "Diana", 160
   "Elaine", 85–88
   "Fuad", 34–35, 39–40, 43–44
   "Guy", 157, 160, 161
   "Ian", 35–36, 40–42, 43–44
   "Janet", 1–13
   "Jim", 149, 150, 159
   "Kelly", 17–29
   "Ken", 136–137, 140–143

"Kevin", 162
keyworkers, departure of, 149–166
"Lilly", 161
"Margaret", 161
"Michael", 16–29
"Miss K", 116–118
"Miss L" 113–116, 118–121
"Mr A", 125–126
"Mr B", 126–128
"Mrs X", 32–34, 37–39, 43–44
"Nick", 156
"Peggy", 137
"Rebeccah", 32–34, 37–39, 43–44
"Robbie" [Alvarez], 58
"Rose", 88–93
"Ruby", 153–155
"Sally", 156, 160
"Sam", 74–82
"Scott", 162
"Simon", 162–163
"Sula", 49–68
"Suzanne", 136, 138, 139
therapeutic home for learning-disabled adults, 134–147
"Will", 135–139
cognitive behaviour therapy, xxii
cognitive development, 96, 142, 144
cognitive functioning:
  effect of organic damage on, 97
  effect of psychotherapy on, xxi
communication(s):
  countertransference, 59
  "niceness" at expense of depth, 130
  non-verbal, 12, 39
  primitive, infant's, 46, 55, 123
  through projection, 123
community learning disability team, 100
Conboy-Hill, S., xix
confidentiality, 20, 30
container/containment, 20, 40, 44, 47, 54–56, 63–68, 106
  internal, fragile, 6

internal skin, 54
maternal, xxv, 55, 68, 117, 121, 130
psychoanalytic theories of, 16, 18, 46, 96, 123, 143
and terror [clinical example: "Janet"], 6–8
contamination, projection of, 58–59
control, as defence mechanism, 24
countertransference, use of, with patients with learning disabilities, xxii, 18, 20, 28, 29, 52, 59, 91, 92, 97, 109
Cowan, C., 170
curiosity, 2, 13, 54, 66, 73, 77, 80, 81, 147, 182
  and desire for knowledge, parent's response to, 72

Dagnan, D., 176
Dalal, C., 166
Davenhill, R., 168
DeAntonio, C., 170
death:
  ability to cope with, 15, 159, 163
  children facing, 14–29
  fear of, 115, 123
defence(s):
  autistic, 53–56, 62
  control as, 24
  denial as, 24, 73
  interpretation of, 26
  against knowledge, 26, 63, 143
  manic, 76
  mechanisms:
    socially structured, 164
    splitting and projection as, 24–25
    used in group process, 24–27
  obsessional, 76
  patients', 16, 114
    challenging, in therapy, 14, 19, 24, 26, 27
  primitive, splitting as, 130
  projection as, 24–25

defence(s) (*continued*):
  psychological, parents', 73, 74, 142
  second-skin, 63
  splitting as, 22, 24–25
denial, 19
  as defence mechanism, 24–29, 73
  omnipotent, 8, 13
"dependence", as basic assumption, 22
depersonalization, 164
depression, 94
  chronic:
    of mother, 16, 46, 145
    of parent(s), 73
development, cognitive: *see* cognitive development
"Diana" [clinical example], 160
difference, confronting, 125
Down's syndrome, 84, 93–95, 99–111, 134
Draw-a-Person test (Goodenough-Harris), 183
dreaming, alpha elements as basis of, 115
drug abuse, 113
Dubinsky, A., 8

echolalia, 102
ego-destructive superego, 84–85, 97
"Elaine" [clinical example], 85–88
Elliott, R., 179
Emanuel, L., xiv, xxiv, 45–68, 180
Emanuel, R., 26, 47
Emerson, P., 157
emotional integration, fluctuating states of, 55
emptiness, 67
  internal, 7
epistemophilic instinct, 72
Evans, J., 24
Evers, C., 170, 175

Faerstein, L. M., 116
Fake, M., ix

Family Relation Test (Anthony & Bene), 181
father, symbolic representation of, 115
feeding difficulties, 46
"fight/flight", as basic assumption, 22
Firth, H., 152
Firth-Cozens, J., 168
Flynn, M. C., 152
Fonagy, P., 179
food, symbolic function of, 40, 43
Forness, S. R., 170
"fragile X syndrome", 75
Frankish, P., 181
Fredman, G., 166
free associations, 118
Freud, S., 43, 46, 71, 72
frustration, 12, 20, 50, 101, 144
  capacity to tolerate, 12, 27, 72, 116
  unbearable, 116
"Fuad" [clinical example], 34–35, 39–40, 43–44

gender identity, 118
good breast, 96
Goodenough-Harris Draw-a-Person test, 181
Gorell-Barnes, G., 31
group basic assumption, 22
"Guy" [clinical example], 157, 160, 161

handicap:
  fluctuating states of, 55
  primary, 55, 88
  secondary: *see* secondary handicap
Harper, D. C., 163
Harris, D. (Goodenough-Harris Draw-a-Person test), 181
harsh superego, 92
Hartland-Rowe, L., xiv, xxvi, 133–148
Hatton, I. H., x

Haviland, J., 145, 147
Henwood, K., 171
Hernandez-Halton, I., 122
Higgit, A., 179
Hobson, R. P., 143
Hodges, S., xiv, xxiii, xxiv, xxvi, 14–29, 167–185
holding environment, 18, 20
"hollow" mental state, 6
Hoxter, S., 4, 63, 142
Hunter, M., 4
Hurley, A. D., 180

"Ian" [clinical example], 35–36, 40–42, 43–44
identification:
  adhesive, 56
  with denying object, 126
institutionalization, long-term, effects of, 113
intelligence, xx, 60
  cognitive, xxi, 181
  constitutional low, 69
  emotional, xxi, 181
  IQ, 69
  organic limit of, xxi
Inter-cultural Therapy Centre (NAFSIYAT), 30
"interdependency of rhythms", 143
interpretations, transference, 91
IQ score, xxi, 69, 70, 183

"Janet" [clinical example], 1–13
"Jim" [clinical example], 149, 150, 159
Jones, G., 155

"K":
  concept of, 47
  function, 98
  reversal of, "–K", 95–97
Kakogianni, M., x, xiv–xv, xxiv, 1–13
Kaufman, S. H., 183
Kelly, G. A., 181

Psychology of Personal Constructs, 181
"Kelly" [clinical example], 17–29
"Ken" [clinical example], 136–137, 140–143
"Kevin" [clinical example], 162
keyworker(s):
  departure of [clinical example], 149–166
  role of, 155–157
Khan, A., 170
Kinetic Family Drawing, 183
King, B. H., 170
Klein, M., 22, 46, 72, 122, 130
knowledge:
  acquisition of, 133–148
  and being alone, 137–138
  and being separate, 138–143
  see also "K"
Kosalowski, B., 143, 144
Krause, I.-B., 31

Lacan, J., xxv, 114, 115
language:
  development, 12
  limited, creative use of, 98–111
  sign (Makaton), 101, 111
learning:
  capacity for
  and early interaction, 133–148
  and therapist's attitude to patient, 83–97
  difficulties, of psychological origin, 69
  disabilities (*passim*):
    women with, therapeutic group for, Tavistock Clinic, 106
  "disability", as term, implications of, xxv, 69–82
Learning Disabilities Service, Tavistock Clinic, xiv, xvi, xix–xxvii, 100, 167–185
Lee, P., xv, xxv, 112–121
Leiper, R., xx, 169, 175
"Lilly" [clinical example], 161

linking, 112
  attacks on, 94

Main, M., 143, 144
Makaton, 101, 111
manic defence(s), 76
Mansell, J., 170
"Margaret" [clinical example], 161
Martin, R. W., 176
masturbation, 52, 64, 74, 109
maternal containment, xxv, 55, 68, 117, 121, 130
maternal reverie, 115, 144
maternal transference, 79, 80
Mattison, V., xv, xvi, xxvi, 149–166
McCormack, B., 18, 26, 28, 29
McCracken, J. T., 170
Meltzer, D.:
  adhesive identification, 62
  "adhesive" relating, 3
  aesthetic impact of mother on baby, 47
  "aesthetic reciprocity", 47–48, 57, 65, 68
  "class of beautiful babies", 66
  Claudia [clinical example], 48–49, 57–58
  "claustrum", 8
  "mental handicap", 54, 55, 69, 73, 110, 149
  fluctuating states of, 55
  as term, replaced by "learning disability", 45, 69
mental health services, audit in, 168
"mental retardation", 70, 75
  as term, replaced by "learning disability", 69
Menzies, I. E. P., 164
"Michael" [clinical example], 16–29
Miller, L., ix, xv, xxv, 83–97, 116
"mirror stage" of development, 114
"Miss K" [clinical example], 116–118
"Miss L" [clinical example], 113–116, 118–121

Money-Kyrle, R., 144
mother(s) (*passim*):
  and baby, primary pre-oedipal relationship between, 83
  depression of, 16, 46, 145
  –infant interactions, and development of thinking, 114–116
  reaction of to handicapped child, 45–68
  receptiveness to infant's projections, 115
"Mr A" [clinical example], 125–126
"Mr B" [clinical example], 126–128
"Mrs X" and "Rebeccah" [clinical example], 32–34, 37–39, 43–44
Muir, E., 143
Murray, L., 143
music therapy, 139
  clinical example, 141

NAFSIYAT (Inter-cultural Therapy Centre), 30
Nagel, B., xx, 169, 175
"nameless dread", 115, 116, 117, 123
narcissistic injury, 31
Nashat, S., xvi, xxv, 112–121
neuroses, 70
"Nick" [clinical example], 156
Nitsun, M., 20
non-verbal children, xxii
  see also language
"normalization", 125

Oakes, P., 177
object, absent, 12
Object Relations test, 183
obsessional defence(s), 76
oedipal conflict, 72, 73
Oedipus complex, 72, 115
omnipotent denial, 8, 13
Orr, R. R., 116
O'Shaughnessy, E., x, 12, 74, 84

Oswin, M., 163
outcome research, Tavistock Clinic Learning Disabilities Service, xxvi, 167–185
project, 182–184

Pahl, J., 151, 155
"pairing", as basic assumption, 22
Papadopoulos, R., 31
Parry, G., 179
paternal transference, 81
Patrick, M., 168
"Peggy" [clinical example], 137
persecutory guilt, 73
Personal Construct Repertory Grids, 182
perverse sense of power, 8
physical contact, 22
  rigid rejection of, 54
  role of, 21
Pidgeon, N., 171
Pistrang, N., xv, xvi, xxvi, 149–166, 179
pleasure principle, 71
"primary disappointment", 47–49
primary handicap, 55, 88
primitive anxieties, 116, 123, 130, 131
primitive communications, infant's, 46, 55
primitive "unintegration", 54
process evaluation, 177–179
projection, 115
  as defence, 24–25
projective assessments, 183
projective identification, 12, 46, 64, 127, 143, 144
projective measures, 180
psychodynamic group therapy, 14–29
Psychology of Personal Constructs [Kelly], 181
psychoses, 70
psychotherapy outcome research, 179–180
psychotic breakdown, manic, 127

quality assurance, Tavistock Clinic Learning Disabilities Service, xxvi, 167–185
Quine, L., 151, 155

Rapley, M., 152
reality principle, 71
"Rebeccah" and X family [clinical example], 32–34, 37–39, 43–44
"recognition" of truth, 144
referrers' survey, 169–171
Reid, S., 20
religion, role of, in therapeutic work, xxiv
religious communities, orthodox, effect on children, 30–44
repertory grids, 181
  measures, 183
reverie, maternal, 115, 144
Reyes-Simpson, E., xvi, xxvi, 122–132
Rhode, M., 102
rhythms, interdependency of, 143
Richard III (Shakespeare), 45–46
"Robbie" [clinical example (Alvarez)], 58
"Rose" [clinical example], 88–93
Rosenberg, M. L., 164
Roth, A., 179
Roy, A., 170
"Ruby" [clinical example], 153–155
Rustin, Margaret, ix, x, 116
Rustin, Michael, 116
Rycroft, C., 27

"Sally" [clinical example], 156, 160
"Sam" [clinical example], 74–82
schizophrenia, 70
Schoenrock, C. J., 176
Scott, B., 116
"Scott" [clinical example], 162
secondary handicap, xx, xxi, xxiii, 64, 68, 70
  defensive exaggerations, 27, 88
  real and inhibiting, 147

secondary handicap *(continued)*:
  resulting from lack of
    containment, 55
  Sinason's head-banging patient,
    63
  Sinason's theory of, 27, 46, 88, 98,
    142
second-skin defences, 63
Seligman, C. K., 176
SENCO (Special Educational Needs
  Co-ordinator), 14, 20
separation, 163
  impact of, 159–166
  managing, 150–166
  mother–child, 81
sexual abuse, 2, 35, 36, 53, 54, 59,
  64, 113
sexual excitement, 51–52
sexual promiscuity, 113
Shakespeare, W., *Richard III*, 45–46
Sheppard, N., xvi–xvii, xxiv, xxvi,
  14–29, 167–185
Shuttleworth, J., 116
sign language (Makaton), 101, 111
"Simon" [clinical example], 162–163
Simons, K., 176
Simpson, D., xvii, xxv, 69–82
Sinason, V., ix, xii, 31, 42, 106, 180
  birthdays in life of person with
    disability, 23
  cognitive vs emotional
    intelligence, 181
  effect of psychotherapy on
    cognitive functioning, xxi
  ethical issues in therapy, 63
  fluctuations in mental capacity,
    140
  "handicapped smile", 36, 161
  head-banging patient, 63–64
  on loss, 110
  "opportunist handicap", 42
  outcome research study, 180, 183
  secondary handicap, xx, xxi,
    xxiii, 27, 46, 63, 68, 70, 98,
    142

  through defensive
    exaggerations, 88
  trauma and loss of birth of
    handicapped child, 142
Skene, R. A., 181
Snowdon, A., 116
social interaction, measures of,
  effect of psychotherapy on,
    xxi
Spanhel, C. L., 176
Special Educational Needs Co-
  ordinator (SENCO), 14, 20
Spillius, E. B., 144
splitting, 64, 131
  as defence mechanism, 22, 24–25,
    130
split transference, 87
Sprince, J., 105, 106
Standen, P. J., 155
Stenfert-Kroese, B., 176
Stern, D. N., 143
stigmatization, social, effects of, 113
Stokes, J., xx, xxi, 55, 180
substance abuse, 113
"Sula" [clinical example], 49–68
superego:
  abnormal, 84
  ego-destructive, 84–85, 97
  harsh and judgemental, 87, 92, 95
"Suzanne" [clinical example], 136,
  138, 139
symbolic function of food, 40, 43
symbolic functioning, 112
symbolic representation of father,
  115
symbolization, 118
Symington, N., xx, 63, 112, 180
Szur, R., 3

Tavistock Clinic *(passim)*
  Adult Department, xx
  Bangladeshi Service, 31
  Learning Disabilities Service, xiv,
    xvi, xix–xxvii, 100, 167–185
Temple, N., ix

terror, and need for containment [clinical example: "Janet"], 6–8
Terry, P., 164
therapeutic alliance, dimensions within, 112–121
therapeutic space, xxv
thinking:
  alpha elements as basis of, 115
  attacks on, 98–111
  development of, 12
  factors affecting, 122–132
  and mother–infant interactions, 114–116
  severe impairment in capacity, 47
third space in psychotherapy, 112–121
transference, 29, 44, 83, 92, 94, 117, 131
  interpretations, 91
  maternal, 79, 80
  paternal, 81
  split, 87
trauma, early, xxiii
Trevarthen, C., 143
"triangular space" within therapy, xxv, 112, 115

Tronick, E., 144
Tustin, E., 54

"unintegration", primitive, 54
Usiskin, J., xvii, xxi, xxiv, 30–44, 105–106, 180, 183

Vineland Adaptive Behaviour Scales, 184
"virtual other", Braten's concept of, 144, 145

Waddell, H., 170, 175
Waddell, M., ix, xi–xii, 116
Wadsworth, J. S., 163
WAIS-III-UK, 183
Waitman, A., xix
Wallace, W., 151
Warden, S., 180
Watts, F. N., 179
"Will" [clinical example], 135–139
Williams, G., x, 6, 12
Winer, J. L., 176
Winnicott, D. W., 18
withdrawal, autistic-type states of, 46

Yanok, J., 163